D0667337

TECHNOLOGY, STRATEGY, AND ARMS CONTROL

Also of Interest

†*Nuclear Strategy, Arms Control, and the Future,* edited by P. Edward Haley, David M. Keithly, and Jack Merritt

Nuclear Non-Proliferation: Congress and the Control of Peaceful Nuclear Activities, Robert L. Beckman

Nuclear Past, Nuclear Present: Hiroshima, Nagasaki, and Contemporary Strategy, Ian Clark

A Strategy for Terminating a Nuclear War, Clark C. Abt

The Environmental Effects of Nuclear War, edited by Julius London and Gilbert F. White

Soviet Nuclear Weapons Policy: A Research Guide, William C. Green

The Soviet Union and Strategic Arms, Robbin F. Laird and Dale R. Herspring

Nuclear Arms Control Choices, Harold Brown and Lynn E. Davis

†*Toward Nuclear Disarmament and Global Security: A Search for Alternatives,* edited by Burns H. Weston with the assistance of Thomas A. Hawbaker and Christopher R. Rossi

Conflict and Arms Control: An Uncertain Agenda, edited by Paul R. Viotti

Global Nuclear Energy Risks: The Search for Preventive Medicine, Bennett Ramberg

Atoms for Peace: An Analysis After Thirty Years, edited by Joseph F. Pilat, Robert E. Pendley, and Charles K. Ebinger

†*Arms Control and International Security,* edited by Roman Kolkowicz and Neil Joeck

†*International Security Yearbook 1984/85,* edited by Barry M. Blechman and Edward N. Luttwak

†Available in hardcover and paperback.

About the Book and Editor

Focusing on the most urgent issues of arms control, this collection of essays discusses the East-West military balance, the nature of U.S.-Soviet relations, the political dynamics of developments in weapons technology, the problems that conflicting national security policies pose for the management of the Western alliance, the influence of U.S. domestic politics on the prospects for arms control, and the efforts to enhance the prospects of peace through peace research. The political, technological, and ethical dimensions of the arms race and of arms control efforts are examined against the background of their historical development in the postwar period and analyzed with a view toward enhancing the prospects for a less volatile military-strategic environment and a more stable international political order. Together these original essays provide a comprehensive overview of the possibilities for and limitations of restraining and managing nuclear issues in the 1980s and beyond.

Wolfram F. Hanrieder is professor of political science at the University of California, Santa Barbara. He is the editor of *Helmut Schmidt: Perspectives on Politics* (Westview, 1982); *Arms Control and Security: Current Issues* (Westview, 1979); *West German Foreign Policy, 1949-1979* (Westview, 1979); and (with Larry Buel) *Words and Arms: A Dictionary of Security and Defense Terms* (Westview, 1979).

TECHNOLOGY, STRATEGY, AND ARMS CONTROL

edited by Wolfram F. Hanrieder

Westview Press / Boulder and London

Copyright © 1986 by Westview Press

Published in 1986 in the United States of America by Westview Press, Inc.; Frederick A. Praeger, Publisher; 5500 Central Avenue, Boulder, Colorado 80301

Library of Congress Cataloging in Publication Data
Main entry under title:
Technology, strategy, and arms control.
    Essays based on lectures delivered at the
University of California, Santa Barbara, Program in
Global Peace and Security.
    1. Armaments—Addresses, essays, lectures. 2. Arms
race—History—20th century—Addresses, essays,
lectures. 3. Arms control—Addresses, essays,
lectures. 4. National security—Addresses, essays,
lectures. I. Hanrieder, Wolfram F.
UA10.T4 1986   327.1'74   85-17861
ISBN 0-8133-0177-7
ISBN 0-8133-0178-5 (pbk.)

Printed and bound in the United States of America

10   9   8   7   6   5   4   3   2   1

CONTENTS

PREFACE

The essays collected in this anthology are based on lectures delivered at the University of California, Santa Barbara (UCSB), during the academic year 1984-1985. The lectures were part of the newly established Program on Global Peace and Security, through which UCSB seeks to augment its existing academic programs with a public dialogue on some of the most pressing problems that stand in the way of achieving a more peaceful and just world order. The primary purpose of this program is to enable our undergraduate students to complete their formal major by pursuing an organized plan of study concerning global peace and security issues and to help them examine these issues from a variety of perspectives—from different academic disciplines, from different political orientations, and from the points of view of different parts of the world. Beyond that, the program aims to reach a wider audience—on and off campus—and foster the reasoned discussion of problems that affect, directly or indirectly, our daily lives and local communities, although their origins and possibilities for solution may be distant in both time and place. Arranging for a series of public lectures, and publishing the essays that resulted from them, is part of this effort.

Avoiding nuclear war is the most urgent task of our age. For this reason, the lectures during the program's first year focused on issues of the East-West military balance, its technological and political dynamics, and its implications for national security policy and arms control. But we do not intend to define the issues of peace and security narrowly. The central theme for the program's second year will be "World Peace and the International Economic Order," in order to address such topics as the North-South conflict, global and regional trade and monetary regimes, and the role of international organizations in strengthening the economic and sociopolitical foundations of peace and security.

It is a pleasure to acknowledge the generous support the Program on Global Peace and Security has received from Dr. Eulah C. Laucks, president of the Laucks Foundation of Santa Barbara; from Provost David Sprecher, UCSB; and from Professor Herbert York, University of California, San Diego, director of the University of California Institute for Global Conflict and Cooperation. Last but not least, we wish to thank our student participants in the program for the sense of excitement and enthusiasm they have brought to our common endeavor. It is to them that this book should be, and is, dedicated.

Wolfram F. Hanrieder
Santa Barbara, California

U.S.-SOVIET NEGOTIATIONS AND THE ARMS RACE: A HISTORICAL REVIEW

HERBERT F. YORK

A historical review of the negotiating positions of the United States and the USSR in several major arms control areas suggests that each side has special and serious problems in dealing with the other. Why is it so hard for the United States and the USSR to negotiate mutually beneficial arms control agreements? The question arises most pointedly in light of the failure of the first Reagan administration to achieve progress on arms control—a failure that I shall not deal with here specifically as it is covered in many of the subsequent chapters. But it applies as well to other attempts—past, present, and future—by the two superpowers to resort to direct diplomatic means to moderate the arms race and help reduce the chances of nuclear war. In my view there are certain important idiosyncrasies in the negotiating positions of both parties that make it particularly difficult for them to reach such agreements. To show what I mean I shall first take a look at the preferred format for arms limitation, the treaty; then deal with arms limitation through unilateral actions; and finally review the historical background of several major lines of arms control negotiations. In so doing I shall draw in part on my experience as a participant in such sessions, particularly in the latest round of the longest-running nuclear-arms control discussions of all: the sporadic twenty-five-year-old effort to achieve a comprehensive ban on nuclear-weapons tests.

ARMS CONTROL THROUGH TREATIES

The arms limitation format most favored by governments, statesmen, and diplomats is the treaty. The principal advantage of a treaty over, say, paired unilateral actions, is that it spells out in detail all the limitations and restrictions to be undertaken, the means to be used for verifying compliance, the duration of the treaty, and the conditions under which it may be terminated. Only by providing such details is it possible to avoid the misunderstandings (which often seem deliberate) that characterize relations between states with strongly differing political systems. Moreover, treaties between the United States and the USSR are developed step by step and in detail by the superpowers themselves. As a result, all of their provisions are carefully tailored to be in the mutual interest of both parties, thus ensuring a higher probability of compliance than in the case of United Nations conventions and other very broad international arrangements.

Conversely, the principal disadvantage of the treaty approach is that negotiation and ratification often take a very long time, during which external events can cause the process to abort. One recent case in point is SALT (Strategic Arms Limitation Talks) II, which was slowed and delayed by a series of such events—Deng Xiaoping's visit to Washington, the controversy over the brigade of Soviet troops in Cuba, the Tehran embassy capture—and finally aborted by the Soviet invasion of Afghanistan. Another case is that of the Comprehensive Test Ban Treaty negotiations during the Carter administration. Internal opponents of the treaty were able to search out and use bureaucratic maneuvers to slow the negotiating process until it too was finally aborted by the same events that killed SALT II.

ARMS CONTROL THROUGH UNILATERAL ACTIONS

The defense programs of all countries involve a continuous stream of unilateral actions, many of which moderate the nuclear arms race. But nearly all of the moderating actions are the result of fiscal, not political, restraints. Occasionally, however, a unilateral restraint is imposed for the sole or principal purpose of moderating the military confrontation or avoiding some particular exacerbation of it.

A particularly interesting and important example was the twenty-year period of restraint imposed by U.S. presidents on the development of antisatellite weapons. The United States, almost from the very beginning of the space age, has used its military space assets—reconnaissance satellites, for example—for a variety of very important national security purposes. From Eisenhower onward, our presidents have concluded that we would derive a net benefit from a situation in which no state had any antisatellite capability. The United States, therefore, was willing to forgo a program to develop such weapons in the hope that the Soviets would follow suit. As a result, proposals arising in the U.S. Air Force and aerospace industry to develop a general-purpose antisatellite weapon were continually rejected.

In the meantime, and despite U.S. restraint, the Soviets launched their first antisatellite experiment in 1968, and they have continued to conduct further tests in an on-again off-again fashion. Finally, in 1977 President Jimmy Carter decided to make a three-pronged response to those Soviet actions: first, to initiate the development of a U.S. antisatellite weapon; second, to explore means for defending satellites against attack; and third, to begin negotiations with the Soviets to forestall all such developments. Beginning at Helsinki in 1978, three negotiating sessions took place; as I mentioned above, they got nowhere. Now both the United States and the Soviet Union have antisatellite programs under way.

Another important unilateral action took place in October 1958 when, after a succession of slowly converging unilateral statements by President Dwight Eisenhower and Premier Nikita Khrushchev, the United States and the Soviet Union both suspended nuclear tests. This moratorium, as it was called, was in essence based on a matched set of unilateral statements in which each party pledged not to test if the other party did not test. The purpose was to create an atmosphere suitable for working out a formal treaty on the subject, and Eisenhower estimated that one year should suffice. The negotiations did not work out, however, and after fourteen months, on 29 December 1959, Eisenhower denounced the moratorium, saying that the United States was no longer bound by it but would not begin testing without giving notice. Three days later, the Soviets denounced it also but said they would not test unless the "Western powers" did so first.

When France tested its first nuclear weapon three months later, Khrushchev took formal and public note of it. Hence, as of that time there was no longer any de jure basis for a nuclear moratorium, but testing did not in fact resume until eighteen months later, when an extensive Soviet series put a final end to the then purely de facto moratorium. Although there were no external legal restraints—formal or informal—on such testing by any party at that time, U.S. official opinion has always held that the United States was in an important sense entrapped by the Soviets. In the words of one high-level White House official, "they used the moratorium to gain a full lap on us" in the cycle of nuclear testing and development. Ever since then, unverifiable moratoria, whether bilateral or not, have found little support in U.S. government circles.

In recent years, the People's Republic of China and the Soviet Union have made frequent unilateral pledges that they would not be the first to use nuclear weapons, and many have urged that the United States also make such a "no-first-use" pledge. U.S. policy has always been to reserve the right to initiate the use of nuclear weapons, particularly in situations in which the conventional balance may be very heavily weighted against it, and so it has always declined to join in such a pledge, whether on a unilateral or a multilateral basis. Another basic argument has been that such a pledge, if unaccompanied by any further, more concrete actions that might really make first use more difficult or less desirable, would be too easily reversed or disregarded.

More recently, a number of Europeans and Americans have proposed that we unilaterally and as a first step either eliminate all so-called battlefield nuclear weapons (such as nuclear artillery) or at least remove them from close proximity to the inter-German border. They argue that the actual use of such weapons for resisting an armed attack would not be to our net advantage, that we can successfully develop and deploy conventional means for resisting such an attack, and that removing such battlefield "nukes" would substantially reduce the probability of nuclear war in Europe. They argue further that the longer-range nuclear systems, which would presumably still remain available after such a first step, would be fully adequate for continuing the state of nuclear deterrence that has persisted for the last thirty-five years.

THE NUCLEAR TEST BAN

The first concrete step toward controlling the nuclear-arms race was the moratorium on nuclear testing that was observed by both the United States and the USSR from 1958 to 1961. Two main factors lay behind this achievement. One was external: Public concern was expressed in increasingly urgent terms, both in the United States and abroad, about the dangers of radioactive fallout from aboveground nuclear tests, aroused largely by the accidental exposures to radioactivity that resulted from the U.S. Bravo test in the Pacific in 1954. The other factor was internal: A deepening concern on the part of President Eisenhower and some of his advisers (and apparently also on the part of Premier Khrushchev and some of his advisers) about where the nuclear-arms race was heading joined with a determination on both sides to find and take a suitable first step in the direction of doing something about it. The moratorium was not the result of a bilateral negotiation; it was supported by nothing more than a pair of matched unilateral public statements to the effect that "we shall refrain from further nuclear-weapons tests if you will."

In President Eisenhower's view the main purpose for declaring a moratorium was to create a political climate conducive to the negotiation of a detailed treaty on the subject of testing. Unfortunately the negotiations became deadlocked at an early stage over an issue that has continued to plague attempts to negotiate such bilateral arms control agreements ever since: The U.S. negotiators were not satisfied with the verification procedures the Soviet negotiators were willing to discuss, and the Soviets in turn charged that the United States was actually interested only in spying and wanted far too much in the way of intrusions on Soviet national sovereignty. The issue revolved around the problem of detecting and identifying underground test explosions. The United States held that the problem could be handled adequately only on the basis of a system of fairly intrusive and mandatory on-site inspections, and the USSR was unwilling to accept any such arrangement.

After negotiations on a treaty had been under way for more than a year, President Eisenhower became dissatisfied with their pace and, partly in response to pressure from critics within his administration, announced that the United States was no longer bound by its pledge not to test but would not resume testing without giving notice. Several days later Premier Khrushchev declared that in that case the USSR was also no longer bound by its pledge not to test but would not begin testing again unless the Western nations did so first. A few months later, in early 1960, France conducted its first nuclear test. Even so, neither the United States nor the USSR resumed testing immediately. Finally, more than a year later, the USSR suddenly initiated a major series of nuclear tests, thus ending the bilateral moratorium.

This action on the part of the USSR has often been cited as an example of Communist perfidy. I believe it was indeed wrong but not perfidious, as no agreement—either tacit or explicit—to refrain from such tests existed at the time. In any case the United States responded quickly with a major test series of its own. Finally, as a result of the alarm produced by the Cuban missile crisis of October 1962, negotiations were resumed, and in 1963 President John F. Kennedy and Premier Khrushchev finessed the problem of how to verify a ban on underground tests by negotiating and signing the Limited Test Ban Treaty, which banned tests in the atmosphere, outer space, and under water but allowed them to continue underground.

Following this qualified success the United States and the USSR continued to explore the possibility of a ban on all nuclear tests, but they were unable to resolve the fundamental issue of verification. Some additional partial measures were eventually achieved, however, including the Threshold Test Ban Treaty of 1974 and the Peaceful Nuclear Explosions Treaty of 1976. In 1968 the closely related and very important Non-Proliferation Treaty as well as a treaty establishing a Latin American nuclear-weapon-free zone (the Treaty of Tlatelolco) were signed. The goal of a comprehensive test ban, however, has remained elusive.

In 1977 President Carter included the negotiation of a comprehensive test ban among his top arms control priorities. By that time the position of the USSR with regard to on-site inspections had evolved to the point at which the Soviets were willing to accept a voluntary form of on-site inspection. At the same time, the U.S. position had evolved to the point at which a carefully hedged form of voluntary on-site inspections (instead of mandatory ones) was acceptable. The Soviets also indicated their willingness to accept a substantial number of specially designed and constructed "national seismic stations" on their territory. Between ten and fifteen of these stations were to be built according to agreed specifications and provided with cryptologic systems that would guarantee that the data stream received from them was continuous and unmodified. The details of a treaty were only about half worked out when external events slowed the negotiations to such an extent that it became impossible to complete the process before the end of President Carter's term. Among the external factors were unanticipated difficulties in the second phase of SALT II, which was going on at the time, the seizure of U.S. hostages in Iran, and the Soviet intervention in Afghanistan. The Carter round of test-ban negotiations was adjourned indefinitely a week after the 1980 elections.

The Reagan administration decided immediately after taking office not to resume the negotiations, but it continued to debate for almost a year and a half its reasons for not doing so. One group argued that the administration should simply declare that as long as the United States relied on nuclear weapons as an important element of its defense strategy, it would be necessary to continue testing them, and so a comprehensive test ban would not be in the nation's interest for the foreseeable future. A second group argued that the main problem was that there still was no adequate system for verifying a ban on underground tests (implying that if there were, the United States might then be willing to negotiate an agreement). The second group eventually won the internal debate; the current official position is that a comprehensive test ban remains a "long-term goal" of the United States, but "international conditions are not now propitious for immediate action on this worthy project."

In recent years, including the entire tenure of the Carter administration, the Joint Chiefs of Staff have consistently and forcefully argued that a comprehensive test ban would not be in the best interests of the United States, whether or not it could be adequately verified (and they did not believe it could be). In particular, they have asserted that as long as the nation maintains a stockpile of nuclear weapons, at least occasional tests will be necessary to assure that the weapons in the stockpile are still in working order. The Joint Chiefs based this position on the advice given to them by their own advisers in the Defense Nuclear Agency (DNA) and on the advice of most of the experts in the nuclear-weapons laboratories. The issue of "stockpile reliability," as it is called, has continued to be the principal basis for Department of Defense opposition to a comprehensive test ban.

The main argument in favor of a comprehensive test ban in recent years has been that it is an essential element of the nation's non-proliferation policy. In particular, it is usually pointed out that the Non-Proliferation Treaty, which has been signed or acceded to by a large majority of the world's nations, calls for "good faith" negotiations by the superpowers to end the arms race and ultimately to eliminate their nuclear weapons, and the seriousness with which they approach the test-ban issue is widely taken as a measure of their good faith in the matter.

The verification issue remains highly controversial. In brief, large- and moderate-yield nuclear explosions can be readily detected and identified by means of remote sensors, but very small ones cannot. The boundary separating the two classes of events is indistinct, however, and that leads to widely varying interpretations of the data, depending on the predisposition of the person interpreting them.

NUCLEAR NONPROLIFERATION

From the beginning of the nuclear age the dominant view in both the United States and the USSR has been that the interests of both countries and indeed of the world would best be served if there were no other nuclear powers, or at any rate as few as possible. This is one of the rare instances in which both the United States and the Soviet Union seem to be fully aware that their interests are exactly parallel. The United States has devised a number of specific policies and actions designed to promote the goal of the nonproliferation of nuclear weapons, sometimes unilaterally and sometimes in concert with other nations. Among the measures taken were the creation of the International Atomic Energy Agency, the passage by Congress of the Nonproliferation Act of 1978, and numerous diplomatic initiatives involving such matters as severely limiting the reprocessing of spent fuel from nuclear reactors and placing restrictions on the sale of nuclear-power equipment. Last but certainly not least is the Non-Proliferation Treaty of 1968, which went into force in 1970.

In essence the Non-Proliferation Treaty can be viewed as an attempt to divide the nations of the world permanently into two categories: one consisting of those nations that already had nuclear weapons and that were pledged not to help anyone else obtain them and the other made up of those nations that did not have nuclear weapons at that time and promised to forgo them forever. In return for the promise not to acquire nuclear weapons the non-nuclear nations exacted two promises from those signatories that already had them. First, the "haves" would help the "have-nots" acquire the technology that would enable them to benefit fully from the peaceful applications of nuclear energy; second, the "haves" would undertake serious negotiations to end the nuclear-arms race and eventually eliminate their own nuclear weapons. The treaty also called for a review of the overall situation every five years. At both of the first two review conferences (in 1975 and 1980) many participating countries complained that neither of the superpowers was living up to the special obligations described above. In spite of these complaints there have been no defections from the treaty; more important, no further nuclear-weapons proliferation has occurred since the treaty was signed.

There are of course cases in which further proliferation could happen soon (India, Pakistan, Israel, South Africa, Argentina, and Brazil, for example), but so far even those countries that have evidently advanced quite far down the road toward a nuclear-weapons capability have refrained from testing or otherwise overtly establishing themselves as nuclear-weapons states. (This observation applies even to India, which exploded a nuclear device years ago but has not created a nuclear-weapons force.) Surely the policies and actions described here, including in particular the Non-Proliferation Treaty, must be viewed as a large part of the reason for the long and quite unexpected delay in the appearance of additional nuclear powers beyond the five that have had a nuclear-weapons force since the People's Republic of China became a member of the club in 1964.

In spite of this generally successful record, some very important nations have refused to sign the Non-Proliferation Treaty, including China, France, Cuba, India, Argentina, Brazil, and Israel. For France and China the omission is particularly serious, but at least each of these countries has pledged to live up to the spirit of the treaty, although refusing for political reasons to adhere formally to it.

STRATEGIC ARMS LIMITATION TALKS: SALT I AND II

President Lyndon Johnson, early in his term of office, proposed a freeze on the further development or deployment of strategic delivery systems. After some discussion of the proposal at the Geneva arms talks, President Johnson met with Premier Aleksey Kosygin in Glassboro, N.J., where they discussed the matter privately. On this occasion Secretary of Defense Robert S. McNamara, who was also present, first formally raised the idea of initiating such a freeze by prohibiting the deployment of antiballistic missile (ABM) systems. Premier Kosygin rejected the idea on the ground that ABM weapons were purely defensive and that it was, after all, only offensive weapons that threatened the lives of many millions of people. Secretary McNamara and other Americans, however, persisted in arguing at various public and private meetings that the development and deployment of ABM systems stimulated the arms race just as much as the development and deployment of offensive systems because of an "action-reaction cycle" in which the development of defensive weapons promoted the development of new offensive weapons. Eventually the Soviets came around to this point of view.

President Johnson's attempts to initiate formal bilateral negotiations on the limitation of strategic arms were thwarted by the Soviet intervention in Czechoslovakia in 1968. Only after Richard Nixon became president in 1969 and the international scene had calmed down was it possible to get the SALT process under way. The first series of these talks, SALT I, concluded in 1972 and resulted in two achievements: a treaty that severely limited the deployment of ABM systems and an executive agreement that temporarily froze the deployment of land-based and sea-based offensive missiles at numbers equal to those already deployed plus those whose deployment was under way at the time the agreement was signed. The net result was a rough strategic balance, intended not as an end in itself but as the basis for further negotiations. The ultimate aim was to produce a situation of actual overall parity at a much lower level of total deployments.

One of the residual problems of the SALT I agreements was that the USSR was left with a substantial number of very large missiles (designated SS-18s by Western sources), whereas the United States had no missiles of comparable size. In the early 1970s, before highly accurate MIRVs (multiple independently targetable reentry vehicles) were fully developed and widely deployed, this imbalance did not seem serious to most observers, but in recent years, with the perfection of high-multiplicity MIRV systems and the achievement of very high accuracies by the USSR as well as by the United States, the issue of the SS-18s has come to be seen as a serious matter. The new developments increase the vulnerability of the land-based component of the U.S. triad (which consists of land-, sea-, and air-based systems), the leg on which U.S. defense policy places the most reliance.

The next step after SALT I was the Vladivostok Accords of 1974, signed by President Gerald Ford and Soviet leader Leonid Brezhnev. The Vladivostok agreement was intended to establish general guidelines for the detailed SALT II negotiations, which had already started in Geneva. The guidelines called for an "equal aggregate limit on delivery vehicles" of 2,400 and an "equal aggregate limit on MIRV systems" of 1,320. The effort to transform the Vladivostok guidelines promptly into a formal treaty ran afoul of both technical and political problems. The technical problems involved the question of how to accommodate cruise missiles and the Soviet Backfire bomber; the political problems arose from increasing disillusionment in the United States about détente and the challenge to President Ford's nomination by the right wing of the Republican party.

In 1977 the SALT II negotiations became the principal element of President Carter's arms control policy. At first President Carter proposed some reductions in the number of deployed systems below the Vladivostok aggregates, a 50 percent cut in the Russian heavy missiles (modern versions of which were barred to the United States entirely), as well as limits on tests, improvements, and numbers of MIRVed intercontinental ballistic missiles (ICBMs). The latter provisions were intended to forestall any further worsening of the problem of ICBM vulnerability and generally reduce technological pressures on the arms race. The USSR, however, insisted on staying within the Vladivostok framework. The SALT II negotiations were completed in Geneva and in a series of high-level meetings over the next two years, and the resulting treaty was signed by President Carter and President Brezhnev in Vienna in 1979.

The SALT II Treaty basically kept the Vladivostok framework. It set an overall limit on strategic nuclear delivery vehicles of all kinds at 2,250 for each side, and within that limit it provided a series of sublimits, setting a ceiling of 1,320 on MIRVed systems of all kinds (including heavy bombers with long-range cruise missiles), a ceiling of 1,200 on MIRVed ballistic missiles, and a ceiling of 820 on MIRVed ICBMs. It also limited each side to only one new type of ICBM, banned major changes in existing systems, and set specific limits on the number of reentry vehicles that could be placed on the one new ICBM and on each type of existing ICBM. In addition temporary limits on ground-launched cruise missiles (GLCMs), sea-launched cruise missiles (SLCMs), and mobile ICBMs were intended to provide time for the negotiation of longer-term agreements on these systems.

Much of the criticism of the SALT II Treaty in the United States grew out of widespread frustration over the nation's international troubles, exaggerated fears of nuclear inferiority (stimulated by right-wing critics at home), and lack of confidence in President Carter's competence in security matters generally and his commitment to military programs in particular. In addition, the impending presidential election made Republican senators reluctant to hand a major foreign-policy victory to a weakened opponent. In spite of broadly based satisfaction with the overall terms of the treaty itself, several particular treaty issues raised serious questions in the minds of those senators and other political figures who took an extremely cautious view of the entire arms control process.

One such issue was that SALT II, like SALT I before it, did nothing to alleviate the heavy-missile problem other than to put a rather high cap on the number of warheads each type of missile could carry. A second issue involved the Backfire bomber, an aircraft that is technically capable of reaching the United States under certain unusual circumstances. Some U.S. observers asserted that the Backfire was therefore an intercontinental bomber that must be included under the ceilings. The USSR contended (and many U.S. observers agreed) that the Backfire's mission was only that of an intermediate-range bomber, and so it should not be included, particularly because the U.S. medium-range aircraft in Europe capable of reaching the USSR had been excluded at Vladivostok over strong Soviet objections. A third issue involved the encryption of certain test data broadcast by Soviet missiles during test flights. This last subject is a rather arcane one that cannot be usefully elaborated in an unclassified discussion. Suffice it to say that most of the professionals who were then involved believed the matter had been adequately handled.

On the Soviet side the principal issue raised after the Vladivostok meeting concerned cruise missiles, which the USSR wanted sharply constrained. (To avoid limitations on their own existing cruise missiles the Soviet negotiators insisted that any limits apply only to missiles with a range of more than 600 kilometers.) The issue took on added urgency with the discussion among the member states of the North Atlantic Treaty Organization (NATO) of the possible deployment of ground-launched versions of such systems in Europe, together with

President Carter's decision to cancel the B-1 bomber and to emphasize the deployment of air-launched cruise missiles (ALCMs) on bombers based in the continental United States.

In the case of long-range ALCMs the principal issue was not a ban but how the missiles were to be counted. Was a bomber carrying ALCMs to be counted as a single delivery vehicle no matter how many missiles it carried (as is the rule for a bomber carrying bombs or short-range missiles), or was each ALCM to be counted as an individual delivery vehicle (as in the case of submarine-launched ballistic missiles)? The Soviet Union finally agreed to a complex compromise counting only the bombers, with certain provisos pertaining to the average number of cruise missiles permissible on all bombers so equipped. Also, if the number of bombers equipped with cruise missiles were to exceed 120, then the number of MIRVed missiles would have to be correspondingly reduced. With regard to ground-launched and sea-launched cruise missiles the United States sought to have no limits applied, because other intermediate-range systems (such as the new Soviet SS-20 missile) were not being limited in the agreement; the USSR wanted a total ban. In any event, testing and development of those cruise missiles were suspended until the end of 1981 in order to allow further negotiations.

Eventually all these issues were resolved to the satisfaction of the two presidents and most of their advisers, but they continued to provide the basis for opposition to the treaty within the U.S. body politic, and as a result the ratification process was delayed. Ultimately, external events—the matter of the "Russian Brigade" in Cuba, the hostage crisis in Iran, and Soviet intervention in Afghanistan—overtook the process and brought the attempt to ratify the treaty to a full stop. Carter administration officials involved in the effort (including myself) remain convinced that for all the trouble the treaty had on Capitol Hill, it would in the end have been ratified but for the Soviet intervention in Afghanistan.

THE MATTER OF CONCESSIONS

There has been a great deal of public discussion in the United States of U.S. concessions—real and imagined—made in the course of postwar arms control negotiations with the USSR. The Western account of these events, however, contains virtually nothing about Soviet concessions, even though the USSR has made a number of important ones. One such concession has to do with the definition of the term "strategic delivery system." It has always been the U.S. position that a strategic delivery system is one that is deployed either in its home territory or at sea and that can reach the home territory of the other country from that deployment site. On the other hand, the Soviet position has always been that a strategic delivery system is a system that is able to reach the other country's home territory from its deployment site no matter where that site is. This difference in viewpoint arises from the very different geopolitical situations of the two superpowers, and it shows up most sharply in the case of "forward-based systems," that is, those medium-range U.S. systems that are currently deployed in Europe and that can reach the USSR only when so deployed. The United States has consistently refused to count such systems in the SALT totals, and the Soviet Union has consistently contended that they should be included.

A second Soviet concession involves the British and French nuclear forces. The USSR contends that the long-range delivery systems of these two NATO countries should be included in the SALT totals. The United States contends that SALT is strictly bilateral and so only the forces of the United States and the USSR should be counted. In the SALT I agreement the Soviets said they would accept the U.S. position provided that the British and French together did not deploy more than nine ballistic missile submarines (more precisely, that the total number of submarines deployed by the United States, Great Britain, and France not exceed fifty).

A third major concession by the Soviet Union involves the procedure for counting ALCMs on U.S. bombers. As long as the total number of these cruise missiles remains less than 3,000 and certain counting rules are satisfied, only the number of bombers so equipped, but not the number of cruise missiles, need be counted and limited under the SALT ceilings. Like the United States in the case of the much more widely reported U.S. concessions, the USSR has apparently made these concessions and others in a serious spirit of compromise in order to produce a mutually beneficial result.

Let me conclude by reiterating my concern over U.S. policy—a concern that I expressed over fifteen years ago, but which has not, it seems to me, lost any of its cogency:

> Why have we led the entire world in this mad rush toward the ultimate absurdity?
> The reason is not that our leaders have been less sensitive to the dangers of the arms race, it is not that our leaders are less wise, it is not that we are more aggressive or less concerned about the dangers to the rest of mankind. Rather, the reasons are that we are richer and more powerful, that our science and technology are more dynamic, that we generate more ideas of all kinds. For these very reasons, we can

and must take the lead in cooling the arms race, in putting the genie back into the bottle, in inducing the rest of the world to move in the direction of arms control, disarmament and sanity. . . .

It may be beyond our power to control or eliminate the underlying causes of the arms race by unilateral actions on our part. Our unilateral actions certainly have determined its rate and scale to a very large degree. Very probably our unilateral actions can determine whether we move in the direction of further escalation or in the direction of arms control and, in the long run, nuclear disarmament.[1]

Since the time when I wrote those words, the balance in who did what first has shifted somewhat. The Soviets have generally caught up with us in numbers of nuclear weapons, and, indeed, even surpassed us in certain particulars, and they introduced a number of novel and important qualitative features into their nuclear arsenal before we did. Despite this shift, I am still inclined to believe that the best hope for a better world lies in our promoting and taking the initiatives necessary for containing the arms race, either unilaterally or in concert with others, as particular circumstances dictate.

NOTES

1. Herbert F. York, *Race to Oblivion: A Participant's View of the Arms Race* (New York: Simon and Schuster, 1971), pp. 238–239.

2

THE NUCLEAR SUPERPOWER RELATIONSHIP: POLITICAL AND STRATEGIC IMPLICATIONS

PAUL C. WARNKE

During the first Reagan administration, statements of high officials, including the president himself, made it clear that arms control was not being given high priority. Instead, the emphasis was on building up U.S. military strength. The president and his secretary of defense, Caspar Weinberger, talked about the need for remedying a "decade of neglect," in which the Soviet Union had allegedly been increasing its strategic nuclear and conventional forces while the United States stood passively by. However unsubstantiated the allegation may have been, it had definite policy implications.

During the election campaign of 1984, and following the president's reelection, a striking change became noticeable in the president's statements with respect to the importance of nuclear arms control and even with respect to the Soviet Union itself. References to the "evil empire" gave way to more conciliatory remarks about working together to avoid nuclear disaster. These more forthcoming pronouncements created a climate in which productive negotiations may take place.

Resumption of the nuclear strategic arms control process came none too soon; in fact, it was about six years overdue. The last agreement on limiting nuclear weapons was signed by President Jimmy Carter and Soviet leader Leonid Brezhnev in June 1979. That agreement, the Strategic Arms Limitation Talks (SALT) II Treaty, was never ratified, and in any event its stated term expires at the end of

1985. There is at present no legally binding agreement in effect to control offensive nuclear arms. The SALT I Agreement expired in 1977, and the limitations of SALT II restrain certain weapons developments only because of the separate statements by the Soviet Union and the United States that each will do nothing inconsistent with the treaty's terms so long as the other side continues to abide by them.

Thus, the arms control regime as it now exists is a very fragile one. The treaty limiting antiballistic defenses is one of indefinite duration. But the program described by some of President Reagan's advisers would involve stationing systems in space that could attack missile warheads and would therefore be inconsistent with specific provisions of the Antiballistic Missile (ABM) Treaty, which is the core of SALT I. Moreover, the construction of a new radar in Siberia—near Krasnoyarsk—may indicate that the Soviet leadership is already positioning itself to deploy nationwide ballistic missile defenses when and if the current treaty is repudiated.

THE NUCLEAR BALANCE

There are some, both in government and outside it, who argue that a period of suspension of arms control negotiations was needed for the United States to build up strategic nuclear forces and then be able to negotiate from a position of greater strength. But the U.S. position has always been one of at least parity with the Soviet Union. Moreover, as the United States builds up, so does the Soviet Union. Neither will let the other gain an advantage. Accordingly, contrary to some contentions, the strategic balance today is no more favorable to the United States than it was in 1980. Both sides have continued to accumulate nuclear arms and both sides, as a consequence, are somewhat less secure in 1985 than they were in 1979, when SALT II was signed.

Many of the new weapons systems that have been much talked about have not yet been deployed. But most of those that have been made operational by one country have been, or are being, matched by the other. The condition of relative parity, i.e., rough equality, persists. But because of greater accuracy and, in some instances, shorter flight time before a warhead reaches its target, the strategic balance is less stable. The retaliatory forces on each side are more at risk because of these increasing counterforce capabilities, and adoption of dangerous strategies, such as "launch on warning," has become a greater possibility.

The United States has, for example, made a substantial start in the deployment in Western Europe of 108 Pershing ballistic missiles and 464 ground-launched cruise missiles. This was done in response to the deployment of Soviet SS-20s, which can strike targets in Western Europe and Asia, though not in the United States. But additional SS-20s are being installed as the U.S. missiles are being put in place in West Germany, the United Kingdom, and Italy. Moreover, the USSR has moved its shorter-range nuclear missiles into Czechoslovakia and East Germany, from which they can strike NATO military installations in the forward areas. In addition, the Soviet Union has increased its ballistic nuclear submarine patrols off the coast of the United States. Pending, but imminent, is the deployment of sea-launched cruise missiles by both countries—relatively small, hard to verify numerically, and capable of being carried on both surface ships and submarines operating just outside of territorial waters.

The U.S. MX (missile experimental) intercontinental ballistic missile has encountered strong congressional opposition because of its cost and because of the inability to devise a basing system that would increase its theoretical chances of surviving a Soviet attack. If it is deployed, however, it is clear that the Soviets will continue with the development and deployment of their SS-X-24, which would be the first big Soviet missile to use solid fuel, like the U.S. ICBMs, and thus instantly ready to launch its ten superaccurate warheads against U.S. targets.

At one point, one of the key Reagan administration officials dealing with arms control expressed his worries about renewed negotiations, stating that things were going smoothly during a period without negotiations. In a sense, he is right. In the absence of negotiations, the arms race has been able to proceed without obstacles. For those who believe that U.S. strength and safety can best be advanced by more and more nuclear arms, this is a comforting thought. But those who believe that safety lies not in more U.S. warheads but in fewer nuclear arms on both sides cannot be convinced that everything has been going smoothly. Instead, we have seen it going sour.

NUCLEAR ARMS AND POLITICAL PURPOSE

The most formidable obstacle to nuclear arms control has been the failure to accept it fully as a national policy and as an essential element in U.S. national security. The debate rages today, as it has in the past, between those who see nuclear weapons as serving strictly to neutralize the nuclear weapons of the other side and those who see them as militarily useful and a means of achieving foreign policy objectives. For nuclear weapons to have other than a deterrent role, however, the United States would have to possess the ability to fight and win a nuclear war.

In the early years of the Reagan administration, the annual reports to Congress of the secretary of defense stressed as an essential purpose of U.S. nuclear arms the ability to prevail in a nuclear war. This theme is no longer being struck. Indeed, in his 1984 State of the Union address President Reagan directed certain of his remarks to the people of the Soviet Union and said, "The only value of nuclear weapons is to make sure they will never be used." I agree wholeheartedly with that statement and hope that it reflects the policy to be followed during the president's second term.

If this is in fact the president's considered view, if he understands and believes this, then he must favor an approach that would preserve mutual deterrence at the lowest possible level of numbers and risk. His declaration as to the only purpose of nuclear weapons is incompatible with any drive for nuclear superiority. If nuclear superiority were the objective of U.S. policy, this, of course, would mean abandonment of any genuine attempt at negotiating arms control—neither side would concede any meaningful advantage to the other at the bargaining table. But if each side recognizes that its nuclear forces can serve only to prevent the use or the plausible threat of the use of nuclear weapons, then arms control can develop and thrive.

Although the major doctrinal illusion is that nuclear superiority can somehow be obtained, other illusions can and do frustrate the arms control process. Closely related is the myth that the Soviet Union can be cowed into giving us arms control by default. The notion is often advanced that the Soviets will be willing to negotiate seriously only when we go ahead with weapons systems that threaten their ability to respond effectively to a nuclear attack. Thus, even such a generally sensible document as the 1983 report of the President's Commission on Strategic Forces (popularly known as the Scowcroft Commission Report) argues that by going ahead with MX deployment the United States can persuade the Soviets to move from large MIRVed ICBMs to a less threatening arsenal of single-warhead missiles known as Midgetmen.

This "arms race theory of arms control" has been tried in the past, with negative results. Premier Nikita Khrushchev boasted in the 1950s of his missile supremacy. He created fears of a missile gap and led the United States to create a real one in its own favor. The argument made for deployment of MIRVed missiles—those with multiple independently targetable reentry vehicles—was that this would give the United States bargaining leverage in the early 1970s.

What it gave instead, in the late 1970s, were Soviet MIRVed missiles that were then said to have opened a "window of vulnerability" for the U.S. land-based ballistic missile force. In its most recent form, the arms race theory of arms control has been used by supporters of the deployment of ballistic missile defenses. The contention is that if the United States goes ahead with systems that can provide even limited protection for its ICBM silos, this will persuade the Soviet Union of the futility of maintaining their large ICBMs and make them receptive to proposals for reductions.

DETERRENCE AND DEFENSE

To evaluate the merits of this argument, it is necessary to consider the entire question of attempted defenses against incoming missiles and warheads. Perhaps the most widely discussed and debated issue in the nuclear field today is the question of the strategic defense initiative program, more widely known as "Star Wars." In March of 1983, the president, in a national speech, shared with the country and the world his vision of a future in which security would no longer depend on the threat of mutual annihilation. His was indeed a most attractive vision. No sane, sensitive human being can be comfortable with the "mutual assured destruction" doctrine, often referred to by its pejorative acronym MAD.

The idea that safety lies in your opponent's recognition that launching a nuclear attack will precipitate retaliation against his own society and people is repugnant. It smacks of genocide. But deterrence is not a concept unique to the field of strategic nuclear policy. U.S. troops in Western Europe and Korea are there to deter attack on U.S. allies. Compliance with criminal law rests in large part on the relative certainty that violation will bring about retribution. And with the present state of defensive technology, mutual assured destruction—MAD—is not a theory but an inescapable fact. If there is a nuclear war between the Soviet Union and the United States, we will destroy one another mutually and no present or foreseeable defense will change that fact. Thus, deterrence should not be denigrated, but strengthened.

In his second debate with Walter Mondale during the 1984 presidential campaign, the president asked, "What if we had a weapon that would render Soviet missiles obsolete?" His subordinates rallied 'round the flag, praising this approach as providing a transition to a defense-oriented world in which the mutual assured destruction theory could be abandoned. There is, of course, nothing new about this dream of a perfect defense. It had considerable support in the

1960s. It is hard to accept the fact that the United States can be destroyed in a manner of minutes and that its security rests on the certainty that the attacker would have committed national suicide.

There have always been those who have opposed limitations on strategic defensive systems. Secretary of Defense Weinberger, in fact, announced that he had never been a proponent of the ABM Treaty. He and other opponents are, of course, entitled to their view. But in promoting that view, no one is entitled to pretend to the American people that the deployment of systems designed to provide limited protection for missiles is a move toward the president's dream of an impermeable shield for the United States and its people. Nothing that can now be developed and deployed can serve as a stepping-stone toward the idyllic world in which nuclear weapons have been effectively neutralized.

No existing or foreseeable technology can render offensive missiles obsolete or protect even a significant fraction of our population from nuclear devastation. The Congressional Office of Technological Assessment noted in 1984 that the prospect of an effective defense was too remote to serve as the basis of public expectation or of national policy. Scientific experts in the field of laser and particle beam devices tell us that current systems cannot be developed into a weapon of enough force to destroy incoming warheads in space. Accordingly, all that can now be done in seeking an alternative to deterrence is to conduct advanced research.

Whether or not the United States should agree to forgo such research is, as I see it, a phony issue. No ban on advanced research is going to be proposed, nor could it be accepted by either side. It would not only be unenforceable, but undesirable. No technical means of verification can see what's going on in a high-tech laboratory or look inside a scientist's brain. Research is desirable to determine whether at some point some technology may emerge that would in fact render offensive nuclear warheads obsolete. Moreover, such research is the only way to avoid the possibility of a rude surprise if Soviet researchers were to come upon something when U.S. scientists weren't even looking. All that is banned in the ABM Treaty is the actual development, testing, or deployment of ABM systems other than those permitted by the treaty. An advanced research program is not affected and the pursuit of such research will not block progress in negotiating arms reductions.

What is prohibited by the treaty, however—and what would be completely inconsistent with any progress toward control of nuclear weapons—is the deployment of defensive systems designed to protect missiles from the retaliatory deterrent of the other side. Although this type of system is not a move away from deterrence or the MAD doctrine and is designed, in fact, to improve deterrence, it would have exactly the opposite effect.

THE ISSUE OF BALLISTIC MISSILE DEFENSE

Even before the Glassboro meeting between President Lyndon Johnson and Premier Aleksey Kosygin in June 1967, efforts were made to persuade the Soviet leaders to discuss the limitation of ABM systems. The Soviet argument, over a period of years, was that defensive weapons were good, offensive ones were bad; therefore, arms control talks should focus only on offensive systems. In the latter part of the Johnson administration, those in national security positions in the United States government tried to explain to Soviet officials that any ballistic missile defense that could be developed could be overwhelmed by increases in the number and the sophistication of offensive systems. The logic of this position was finally accepted, and the eventual result was the treaty limiting ABMs. As signed in 1972, it permitted two ABM installations for each country; later it was amended to allow only one per side. The one U.S. installation was built in Grand Forks, North Dakota, and promptly put in mothballs as useless.

For some inexplicable reason, those same discredited arguments for ABM defenses are now being presented again. And even more incredible is that they are being made not by the Soviets but by the United States. U.S. officials today, like Soviet officials in the late 1960s, say that ballistic missile defenses, though imperfect, will be stabilizing, that they will promote, rather than preclude, the limitation and reduction of offensive weapons. But these arguments are just as wrong when made by the United States as they are when made by the USSR. The deployment of strategic defenses designed to knock off some percentage of incoming warheads, but incapable of knocking off all warheads, will just mean more warheads deployed against U.S. targets.

A logical analysis of the merits of attempted ballistic missile defenses requires that we try to understand how this deployment almost certainly will be viewed by the other side. As I mentioned earlier, until that happy day when technology enables construction of an impermeable astrodome over the country and people of the United States, U.S. security rests on an assured and recognized ability to respond with devastating force to any nuclear attack the Soviet Union can launch. Soviet planners recognize that their security similarly depends on their retaliatory capability. If the Soviets see the United

States as building the kind of defense that present technology makes possible, while offensive weapons remain virtually uncontrolled, they could only view this as an attempt to gain a first-strike option. The inevitable Soviet response will be to build up more offensive warheads, with decoys, dummies, and chaff that can overwhelm any system that can presently be put in place. Neither the Soviet Union nor the United States is going to cooperate in giving the other the means of conducting or threatening a preemptive strike.

Those in charge of the president's strategic defense program are honest enough to concede that the utility of any current plans depends on a drastic reduction of Soviet warheads. Put another way, offensive nuclear arms must be substantially cut back before any defensive system can have any chance of success. But if the priority is placed on strategic defense, the prospects of limiting strategic offense are nonexistent.

If defensive systems won't work, why should the Soviets want to block them? The Soviets know that it will be tough and expensive to match any defense the United States creates as well as to devise and deploy the countermeasures that would make U.S. defenses useless. I think the United States convinced the Soviets fifteen years ago that the net result of these steps would mean less security, more risk of a first strike in a time of major crisis. The United States should not forget this: In the nuclear age, insecurity for one side means insecurity for both.

TOWARD NUCLEAR STABILITY

What then are the chances of limiting offensive systems and starting a move toward greater rather than less strategic stability? In my opinion, acceptance of certain basic propositions can bring about major progress.

The first is that an arms race in space cannot possibly benefit the United States. It can be made clear to the Soviets that no existing or proposed agreements will be allowed to prevent the continuation of a research program designed to explore the frontiers of technology in the hope that at some time a system or systems able to neutralize nuclear weapons may be developed. But nothing can be gained by deployment now of imperfect and porous kinds of devices that won't protect people, and that can provide only an imperfect and permeable defense for missiles. Any deployment of this second type of strategic defense should be agreed upon and can safely be agreed upon only when offensive weapons have been drastically reduced.

Nor is there anything to be gained for U.S. security in continuing and accelerating a competition in the development of antisatellite weapons. The United States is more dependent on high-altitude satellites for both peaceful and passive military uses than is the Soviet Union. The provisions of the Outer-space Treaty prohibit both sides from stationing weapons of mass destruction in space, and there is no purpose in perfecting the ability to destroy the permitted types.

Here again, as with limits on ballistic missile defenses, a ban on antisatellite weapons is not a Soviet idea. At the initiative of the United States, talks on prohibiting antisatellite systems (ASATs) were begun in June of 1978. They ought to be resumed and, in the meantime, a moratorium placed on further testing of these unnecessary and destabilizing weapons. If instead both the United States and the Soviet Union perfect sophisticated antisatellite systems and if, for example, satellites needed for early warning were to begin to disappear at a time of crisis, the result could be the triggering of a nuclear war.

A second important conclusion is that a comprehensive and effective arms control approach requires a freeze on further testing and deployment of particular kinds of offensive weapons. As a first step, the United States should propose a ban on any new ICBM with multiple independently targetable reentry vehicles. This would be the best possible use of the MX: Bargain it away in return for Soviet abandonment of its SS-X-24 and any other new MIRVed ICBM. Another system inimical to U.S. national interests is the sea-launched land attack cruise missile. The long U.S. Atlantic and Pacific coasts are, for the most part, a strategic military advantage to the United States. But in an age in which every submarine and surface ship would have to be viewed as a cruise missile carrier, U.S. vulnerability to this type of weapon would be even greater than that of the Soviet Union.

Ironically, the only way currently available defensive technology could be deployed without fueling an arms race would be if deployment were preceded by a freeze on most new offensive weapons. The effectiveness of any attempted defense would depend on prior reductions in existing offensive weapons. The speedy completion of a comprehensive test ban would do much to impede both development of destabilizing weapons and the proliferation of nuclear arms. If the United States and the USSR were to stop all nuclear testing, the certainty of world condemnation would face any other country that initiated the test explosion of nuclear devices.

Another element in a successful arms control approach would be to use the foundation that has already been negotiated in the SALT

I and SALT II talks. SALT II was designed to facilitate further steps in controlling and reducing nuclear weapons. Often overlooked is the fact that the treaty set in place not only an overall limit on the number of strategic weapons but also subceilings on the categories that are of greatest concern. Under the treaty, there is a subceiling on the combined total of submarine-launched and land-based strategic missiles with multiple warheads and a lower subceiling on the MIRVed land-based ICBMs. This is the category in which the Soviet Union has almost 80 percent of its strategic weapons; and a still lower ceiling limits the heavy missiles that only the Soviet Union has.

In addition, a new warhead ceiling needs to be negotiated as an overall limit on all Soviet weapons that can strike NATO territory in Western Europe or North America and all U.S. weapons that can strike the Soviet Union and the Warsaw Pact countries. Such an agreement would cover Pershings, cruise missiles, and Soviet SS-20s. All of these ceilings should be subjected to annual reductions of as much as 10 percent. In my opinion a proposal of this kind would elicit an interested response from the Soviet leadership. The format is one with which they are familiar, and no dramatic new approach would have to be explained and rationalized.

THE NEED FOR ARMS CONTROL

But the basic question that has to be answered before any approach can succeed is whether the United States is really interested in nuclear-arms control. There are, I regret to say, some Reagan administration officials who view negotiations as strictly a political ploy; something that has to be done in order to keep U.S. allies reasonably satisfied and U.S voters reasonably quiescent. For political reasons, therefore, they are prepared to go through the motions in the confidence that if a real agreement threatens it can always be blocked. I am convinced, however, that there are those in the Reagan administration who accept the inexorable logic of nuclear arms—the fact that they cannot be used to win a military victory or to gain political objectives; that their only purpose, as the president has put it, is to make sure that nuclear weapons are never used.

To reach these conclusions, and to consider nuclear-arms control an essential component of U.S. national security, is not to be naive or trusting. If the United States was certain it could really trust the Soviet Union, there would be no need to worry about arms control. If the United States and the Soviet Union shared the same world view, the same objectives for the developing nations, and were friends, then the prospects of nuclear war would be too remote to warrant extended thought. We could turn, instead, to the problems of inequality, poverty, famine, and the other ills that continue to beset mankind. But because we are not friends but rivals, because of the seeming inevitability of frictions and crises in the years ahead, we have to be unwaveringly conscious that confrontation can lead to conflict and conflict can lead to nuclear war—unless the nuclear arsenals are subjected to drastic restraints. The resumption of nuclear-arms talks and the prompt completion of new nuclear-arms agreements cannot guarantee world peace and prosperity. But at least it will give us all the chance, the time, and the resources to continue to work for these objectives.

3

INTEGRATING ARMS CONTROL IN EUROPE: PROBLEMS AND PROSPECTS

JONATHAN DEAN

Positive public reaction in Western Europe to the resumption of U.S.-Soviet arms control discussion cannot conceal the fact that concern over the state of East-West arms control and over the Western strategy of nuclear deterrence has continued. Although antinuclear groups in Western Europe no longer appear capable of fielding the huge demonstrations of 1982–1983, antinuclear sentiment continues strong in the West European public. Indeed, in one sense, there is no need for continuing public activity by the antinuclear movement in the Federal Republic of Germany (FRG), the country of its greatest strength, because its program has largely been adopted by the opposition Social Democratic and Green parties.

The fragmentation of the defense consensus of the past twenty years through the falling away of the British Labour party and the German Social Democrats is a serious blow to NATO (the North Atlantic Treaty Organization), equivalent in long-term importance to the withdrawal of France from the NATO integrated military structure. Impelled by doubts and fears over nuclear weapons, the progressive decline in the confidence of the European public in U.S. security policy continues to cut deep into U.S. influence in Europe. Denmark and Norway already prohibit stationing of U.S. nuclear weapons on their territory, and the Spanish and Greek governments have taken positions pointing to future prohibition. If present trends continue in the Central and Northern Tier of NATO Europe—the Federal

Republic of Germany, Great Britain, Netherlands, Belgium, Denmark, and Norway—there is a considerable possibility that sometime within the next decade one or more NATO governments will formally advocate measures of unilateral nuclear disarmament for itself and for the NATO alliance in general.

In West Germany, the key country for the defense of Western Europe, none of the suggestions for lowering NATO's reliance on nuclear weapons by improving conventional forces have found broad public support. Despite its many military shortcomings, NATO's existing posture of forward defense and flexible response will continue because no other approach can gain more support. Partial improvements will be made in the area of conventional capabilities, but they will be limited by sluggish economies, by the rising cost of armaments, and by mounting taxpayer resistance. This situation may elicit further moves in the U.S. Congress to reduce the U.S. defense commitment in Europe in some way. In addition, controversy over stationing chemical weapons and over space defense programs will contribute importantly to opinion trends in Germany and elsewhere in Europe that are critical of U.S. and NATO defense policies.

Concluding East-West arms control agreements could provide some answer to these trends in Western European public opinion as they might reestablish the European consensus for the two-track "defense-dialogue" policy toward the Soviet Union, which is the logical approach for both Western Europe and the United States. They could also restore public confidence and support in Europe for the second track of negotiated East-West agreements in place of the present slide toward unilateral actions. Once achieved, arms control agreements can stabilize the enormous NATO–Warsaw Pact military confrontation in ways less expensive than force buildup and less likely to further the competitive dynamic of force improvements on both sides. Despite NATO's political problems, the alliance has at its disposal formidable and growing armed forces, enough to provide motivation for the Soviet Union to consider arms control agreements.

The ideal, of course, would be some reformulation of Western policy that would combine fresh approaches to defense and to arms control in an integrated concept of such compelling logic and common sense that it could both restore the Western defense consensus and lead to Soviet acceptance of its arms control aspects. What can be done about moving toward this ideal outcome?

PROSPECTS FOR CURRENT NEGOTIATIONS

U.S.-Soviet nuclear negotiations on intermediate-range nuclear armaments were resumed in early 1985. But the odds against their culmination in a fully articulated agreement in the late 1980s appear considerable. Among the problems are (1) continuing difficulties in U.S. decision making on arms control; (2) a congealing of Soviet decision making on arms control caused by leadership problems and by poor U.S.-Soviet relations; (3) the fact that an agreement to reduce offensive missiles, separate from an agreement covering antisatellite systems (ASATs) and defense, seems unachievable, which exacerbates the difficulty of achieving a negotiated outcome; and (4) the difficulty of agreeing on the stiffer verification provisions that will be a U.S. requirement for concluding any U.S.-Soviet agreement on reducing nuclear weapons.

Two arms control negotiations covering European subject matter are now in progress. The first is the NATO–Warsaw Pact force reduction negotiations in Vienna, now in their eleventh year (their acronym, MBFR, is derived from the Western designation of these talks as negotiations on Mutual and Balanced Force Reductions); the second is the Stockholm Conference on Confidence- and Security-Building Measures and Disarmament in Europe, commonly called the Conference on Disarmament in Europe (CDE), which began in January 1984 among the thirty-five signatory states of the 1975 Helsinki Accords of the Conference on Security and Cooperation in Europe (CSCE).

But even though the subject matter of the INF (intermediate-range nuclear force) talks is being covered in a new forum, the pattern of arms control negotiation affecting Europe will remain a crazy-quilt hodge-podge. Large segments of the huge military confrontation in Europe are left uncovered. There are no negotiations that might reduce their potential to ignite general conflict, and no negotiations are aimed at limiting their contribution to the costly dynamic of competitive force improvements on both sides. The only aspects of this confrontation now being actively negotiated with any prospect of agreement within the next three to four years are modest reductions in military manpower and a few confidence-building measures of limited scope.

If achieved, such agreements would of course be valuable, but they would hardly reach to the core of the huge NATO–Warsaw Pact military confrontation. Even if they should succeed, the two sets of negotiations, MBFR and CDE, are partly overlapping, uncoordinated, and at cross purposes. More important, there is no coverage in the East-West negotiations of Soviet and U.S. tactical nuclear warheads intended for ranges under 1,000 kilometers (these probably reach a combined total of some 15,000—taking into account those deployed in Western Europe by the United States and in Eastern Europe and the western USSR by the Soviet Union), nor of the aircraft, ballistic missile, and artillery delivery systems for these warheads in the hands of the two superpowers and of their allies.

There is also little prospect of active negotiation on reducing conventional armaments in Europe. This is what the Soviets have urged in the MBFR talks, but NATO participants have been strongly opposed. They argue that reduction of armaments of West European NATO participants might put them at a disadvantage with the USSR, as the USSR would not be subject to armament limitations on its western border territory, within striking distance of Central Europe. Finally, although Warsaw Pact and neutral participants have made such proposals, it is unlikely that the present Stockholm CDE negotiations will lead to measures restricting the geographic area or type of force deployments, even though restrictions of this kind could help stabilize the NATO–Warsaw Pact confrontation. To the contrary, there are strong expansionist tendencies in the present military confrontation. The Soviet Union has deployed a large number of SS-20s with a warhead total far exceeding that of the earlier Soviet SS-4s and SS-5s. NATO in turn has deployed U.S. INF missiles, and the Soviet Union has moved modernized Scaleboard SS-22 missiles into Eastern Europe and has modernized its shorter-range nuclear missiles (the SS-21s and SS-23s) already deployed there. All this has added to the nuclear capability of both sides in Europe. Moreover, a new generation of longer-range conventional weapons with highly destructive terminally guided warheads will probably be introduced by both sides in the coming decades. This force modernization will increase the potential gains from preemptive strikes on airports, nuclear-weapons sites, and command centers and place the conventional forces of both sides on hair trigger.

In considering the possibilities for an integrated program I shall look first at the two currently convened negotiations on East-West arms control, CDE and MBFR. Both of these negotiations are multilateral, with many participants in addition to the United States and the Soviet Union. The Stockholm participants, the signatories of the 1975 Helsinki Accords, are all the members of NATO and of the Warsaw Pact and include as well twelve nonaligned and neutral European states, among them Austria, Finland, Sweden, Switzerland, and Yugoslavia. Participating in the Vienna talks are all the members of the NATO alliance except France, Spain, Portugal, and Iceland, and all members of the Warsaw Pact.

One reason for looking at these multilateral negotiations is that they may, during the next four or five years, produce an agreement— the prospects being better for CDE than MBFR—on controlling nuclear weapons. In fact, there may be more momentum in these negotiations than in those on the nuclear level, in part at least because of their multilateral character. Instead of the wary stiffness of bilateral nuclear-arms control talks between the superpowers, multilateral East-West negotiations often have a more amicable and productive ambiance. The respective allies of the two superpowers press each toward accommodation and, with or without agreement of their superpower ally, busily explore alternative moves that it might be illicit to even mention in the more tightly controlled framework of bilateral superpower negotiations. For the United States, multilateral negotiation also has the politically important advantage that allied negotiators can experience firsthand the positions taken by the Soviet Union—often rather negative ones—without the uneasy feeling that U.S. bilateral negotiators are leaving out something, some clue or opening, when they report to their allies, however frequent and detailed these reports may be. Sometimes there is a real basis for this uneasiness: The valuable "Walks in the Woods" compromise solution for the Geneva INF talks, drafted by the U.S. and Soviet chief negotiators, could never have been dismissed summarily by both sides, as it was, if allies of both had been participating directly in the Geneva talks.

Participation by allies also ensures that allied governments will be seen by their own publics to share responsibility for the outcome of the negotiations, something that did not take place with the INF talks, to the serious detriment of U.S. standing in Western Europe following the breakdown of the talks. Beyond these general structural aspects of multilateral negotiation, the allies of the two world powers see special reasons for pressing the agreement on European arms control in the current state of tension between the United States and Soviet Union, even though, in times of closer U.S.-Soviet understanding, allies have often urged a more conservative negotiating stance on the United States to counteract tendencies toward a U.S.-Soviet condominium.

For the West, the process of allies influencing their respective superpower partners has been especially evident in the case of the Stockholm CDE: The allies first brought a reluctant United States to agree to discuss the idea of such a conference and then to agree to actually hold it under terms that foresee a continuation. The process of NATO allies pressing the United States into action has continued during the first year of the conference and has contributed to U.S. acceptance of the inclusion of a commitment on the non-use of force in the event a Stockholm agreement should materialize.

The Warsaw Pact allies, although markedly less influential with the Soviet Union, nonetheless wish to see East-West agreements concluded. The pressures of their weak economies and their conviction that they have more political latitude in their relations with the Soviet Union in periods of good U.S.-Soviet relations is a powerful motive. The Soviet Union has reasons of its own to reach agreement in this multilateral context: It desires to appear conciliatory to the Western European states while stressing claims of U.S. responsibility for the poor state of East-West relations, in order to decrease U.S. influence in Western Europe. When the West Europeans and East Europeans pull in the same direction, they exercise considerable leverage. Although the Soviet Union is less open to such persuasion than is the United States, when all major participants of a multilateral negotiation line up in support of some specific course of action, the Soviet Union takes it seriously.

Beyond these general characteristics of multilateral East-West negotiations, the Stockholm conference has the inestimable advantage of an agreed deadline, in the form of the CSCE review conference set for November 1986 in Vienna, where the Stockholm participants will have to report on their progress. Taken together, these factors come close to assuring that the Stockholm talks, although still in a preliminary stage, will culminate in an agreement by November 1986.

THE PROSPECTS FOR CDE

Nonetheless, progress has been slow in CDE. The first months of the CDE were spent in presentation and justification of proposals by participants; only in November 1984 was agreement reached on procedures for more detailed examination of proposals by establishing two working groups.

At the outset, in January 1984, the NATO states jointly proposed a program of confidence-building measures.[1] Essentially, these NATO proposals represented an expansion and tightening of the Helsinki Accord provisions on notification of military exercises, extending them to cover all out-of-garrison activities and requiring longer advance notice of such activities. Three of the six Western proposals dealt directly with this topic: (1) exchange of information among participants on their military forces, providing unit designation, location, and strength of units down to brigade or regiment level; (2) exchange of annual forecasts of military activities, including exercises and other out-of-garrison movements, over the size of 6,000 men or a combination of units composing the combat elements of a division; (3) notification, forty-five days in advance, of all out-of-garrison activities of forces of the size just specified; (4) a requirement that states invite observers to out-of-garrison activities and some alert activities; (5) verification, consisting of noninterference with national technical means and a limited number of inspections per year on the territory in Europe of participants to test compliance with the other confidence-building measures; and (6) improved communications, hot lines, etc. among conference participants on a bilateral basis.

The six proposals put forward by the Soviet Union and Warsaw Pact participants in their draft treaty of May 1984 were of a different character from these specific, rather limited Western confidence-building measures. The Pact proposals called for general political commitments on (1) non-use of force by participants against each other; (2) prohibition on the first use of nuclear weapons; (3) nuclear-weapons-free zones; (4) mutual reduction of military budgets; and (5) a ban on chemical weapons in Europe; but they also included (6) expansion of the Helsinki measure on prenotification of exercises, including restrictions on the size of land maneuvers and greater precision on prenotification of troop movements, and practices for invitation of observers to maneuvers. The Soviets have also mentioned in general terms the possibility of further steps to decrease the risk of surprise attacks and to promote visits by military personnel. At the end of the spring 1984 round, the nonaligned countries presented some generally worded concepts calling for constraints on military activities, such as limiting the size of maneuvers and the establishment of zones of restricted military activities.

During the first months of the conference, NATO participants criticized the Warsaw Pact program of political commitments as purely declaratory, potentially misleading to Western publics, and lacking real substance in the form of specific commitments. They urged participants instead to focus on their more detailed confidence-building measures. Behind the scenes, the Soviets pressed strongly for a positive Western reaction to their proposal on non-use of force. European NATO participants, interested in a positive outcome of the CDE talks, urged Western acceptance of this concept as a part of the Western position at Stockholm. What they appeared to have had in mind was a potential compromise, with the NATO participants agreeing to include in an agreement a commitment on non-use of force in return for Warsaw Pact agreement to specific confidence-building measures proposed by the NATO participants. In their Washington Declaration of 31 May 1984, the NATO participants hinted at this possibility, and in his speech in Dublin on June 4 President Reagan offered inclusion of a non-use of force commitment if an otherwise satisfactory agreement could be reached.

Up to the end of 1984, Warsaw Pact participants did not show interest in a compromise of the kind just described. However, the essential components of the content of a first CDE agreement were already on the table at Stockholm. Aided by the November 1986 deadline and the supporting elements described above, and in the absence of any flare-up of problems in East-West relations in the intervening period, it is quite likely that the summer and fall of 1986 will see conclusion of a first CDE agreement containing a commitment on the non-use of force and most of the confidence-building measures proposed by the NATO participants.

Of the NATO proposals advanced in Stockholm, the fate of the proposal for inspections is uncertain. The Warsaw Pact participants are prone to argue that inspections should be linked only to force reductions and residual ceilings and should be dealt with in the MBFR talks and applied only in the smaller MBFR area of reductions—the territory of the Federal Republic of Germany (FRG) and the Benelux states in the West, plus that of the German Democratic Republic (GDR), Poland, and Czechoslovakia in the East.

NATO participants at CDE, especially the United States, have made a strong distinction between measures providing for broader exchange of information and measures placing restrictions or "constraints" on military activities. They have argued that all proposals of the latter kind should only be considered in a follow-on conference, CDE Phase II, after there has been an opportunity to evaluate the actual operation of confidence-building measures in a first CDE agreement. Nonetheless, one constraint proposed both by Warsaw Pact participants and neutrals, a measure calling for some numerical limitation on the size of out-of-garrison activities by ground forces, is acceptable to some NATO participants and may in the long run be included in a first agreement. A measure of this kind, which could prohibit the force concentrations that often precede attack, could be useful, depending on whether it actually covers troop movements in a comprehensive way.

It is possible and desirable that some provision for consultation among participants be included in a first CDE agreement. This might be an arrangement for a consultative commission, meeting periodically; or, at the very least, consultations in the event of suspicion of noncompliance, as was suggested by some neutrals. Some NATO participants have opposed a standing commission, fearing it could provide a forum for Soviet propaganda on the entire spectrum of NATO defense activities in Europe. But there is no reason why the Soviet Union should have one-sided use of such a body for propaganda purposes. Western participants could make at least equally good use of a standing commission to comment on defense developments in the Soviet Union and Eastern Europe.

Assuming agreement in Stockholm on the basis described here, what would be the military significance of a first CDE agreement and its implications for the future? Could a CDE Phase II be used as the vehicle for integrating arms control negotiations in Europe? This first CDE agreement would contain no reductions, no limitations on the size of forces, and, with the possible exception of a limitation on the size of out-of-garrison activities, no restrictions on military activities. It would make no direct contribution to slowing down the NATO–Warsaw Pact arms race. The competition in modernized armaments would remain wholly unrestricted.

Moreover, Western proposals suspended the requirement for pre-notification and presence of observers in the initial stages of alerts, an exception that is important to commanders on both sides who wish to continue testing the state of readiness of their forces. Additional exceptions may be requested for troops in transit from other areas via Europe to third areas. Both exceptions would create a big loophole in the coverage of these measures, even though, in the case of alerts, the time period for suspension of coverage may be limited to thirty-six hours or so. A good deal of preparation for surprise attack could take place during one of these unannounced alerts. The potential damage could be limited if the number of alerts fell under a general limitation. Moreover, depending on the comprehensiveness of the definition of out-of-garrison force movements used in an agreement, various types of movements could remain uncovered. NATO forces, configured for largely static defense, would benefit more than Warsaw Pact forces, which are organized for massive, forward-moving attack, from a comprehensive restriction on force concentration. Even the violation of such a restriction by the Warsaw Pact would add to NATO warning, although some Western officials argue that comprehensive constraints on out-of-garrison activities could prevent NATO forces from moving to preparedness positions.

Some neutral countries have proposed a second possible constraint on out-of-garrison activities, prohibition of maneuvers in border areas, which would limit threatening maneuvers of the kind carried out by the Soviet Union along the Polish border in 1980–1981 in connection with the Solidarity development in Poland. Such a measure, which would also introduce in a general sense the concept of zones of restricted activity or deployment, could have a useful psychological effect. But it encounters the objections just noted and exacerbates one of the fundamental problems of NATO defense, the shallowness and lack of defensive depth of NATO territory (with only a few hundred kilometers from the front line to the ports of the Low Countries at its narrowest) as compared with the greater geographical depth of the Warsaw Pact territory. A possible answer would be to have a deeper belt on the Pact side, but this could be negotiated, if at all, only in a configuration that permits alliance-to-alliance negotiation between members of NATO and the Warsaw Pact, rather than an approach that argues for equal treatment for all thirty-five signatories of the Helsinki Accords and disregards the great differences in their geographic situations and the size and importance of their armed forces. I shall return to this below.

A first CDE agreement along the lines sketched here would provide both sides with useful additional information regarding departure from normal military activities of preparation for combat. An agreement that contained a consultation provision would have some possibilities of future growth, and its operation would require a center for coordination of information that could in time develop into some form of East-West crisis-control center. The impact of a first CDE agreement on Western public opinion is bound to be limited, but it would at least partially satisfy public desires in Europe for progress in arms control. Moreover, success in early Stockholm conferences would most likely be followed by a series of future conferences on European security over coming decades. Given this probability, it is essential to begin considering the possible content of a CDE Phase II and even beyond, through long-term planning that would make serious use of the potentialities of such future negotiations.

THE SITUATION IN MBFR

The situation of the Vienna MBFR talks is more problematical than that of CDE. For the last ten years, since the Warsaw Pact in 1975 presented data on its forces in Central Europe that the NATO participants considered incomplete, the MBFR talks have been held up by the dispute between NATO and the Warsaw Pact over the number of Warsaw Pact forces in Central Europe, with NATO estimating these forces at about 180,000 more than shown in Eastern figures for Warsaw Pact ground-force personnel. Yet, over the years, a large number of points needed for an MBFR accord have been agreed in principle between East and West. They include a number of specific measures designed to verify compliance with residual force ceilings after reductions and to reduce the risk of surprise attack, measures that Warsaw Pact participants have accepted in Vienna even though they as yet remain unwilling to discuss similar measures in Stockholm. Many of the considerations applying to the Stockholm talks, especially the multilateral dynamic, apply also to the Vienna talks; and, given the areas of agreement already mapped, they could result in a treaty relatively quickly once the data issue is resolved.[2]

Agreement in principle has already been reached in Vienna on many components of a first MBFR treaty. These include (1) agreement on the long-term goal of reducing ground-force personnel to a 700,000-man ceiling equal for both alliances, with a 900,000-man combined common ceiling for the total ground- and air-force manpower of each alliance; (2) initial reductions of U.S. and Soviet personnel in the general range of 10,000 to 20,000 respectively; (3) a residual ceiling on Soviet and U.S. ground-force personnel and a freeze on the remaining personnel of each alliance; (4) further reductions by all participants on an agreed timetable; and (5) associated measures designed to verify residual ceilings and provide assurance against surprise attack, including prenotification of entry into the area of larger numbers of personnel (20,000 to 25,000), use of exit-entry points manned by military personnel of the other side for those entering or leaving the area, prenotification of out-of-garrison activity of division-size forces (the presence of observers at these movements has not yet been agreed), exchange of information on forces remaining in the area following reductions (the scope of such exchange remains to be agreed), inspections by forces of the opposing alliance (although specific conditions under which inspections would take place remain an important open issue), and a consultative process.

A first agreement on this basis would result in withdrawal of two Soviet divisions from Central Europe; freeze NATO and Warsaw Pact military manpower at its present level; and institute a set of verification measures that would offer more precision, accuracy, and control (although in a smaller area) than that envisaged for CDE Phase I. Although a first MBFR agreement should not be held up for this purpose, the MBFR format can also handle armament reductions, including reduction of tactical nuclear weapons—a proposal (later withdrawn) that the Western participants made in 1975.

As noted, the continuing dispute over the number of Warsaw Pact ground- and air-force personnel stationed in Central Europe has been a major obstacle to an MBFR agreement. Among several possibilities of resolving this dispute are (1) further exchange of more detailed, updated data on Warsaw Pact forces and comparison of the data of NATO and the Warsaw Pact on the same types of Warsaw Pact unit, thus identifying for more detailed discussion major areas of difference; and (2) temporary suspension of the current NATO requirement for prior agreement on data for Warsaw Pact forces for the purposes of a limited first U.S.-Soviet reduction, followed by an attempt to resolve the data dispute on the ground through inspections rather than at the negotiating table.

What is needed to bring about one of these possible solutions is more high-level political interest on both sides in an outcome. With that interest, the Vienna talks could produce a first agreement within a year. Thus far, many leaders on both sides have appeared to consider that East-West agreement to reduce military forces in an initial MBFR accord, however modest in scope, would constitute a serious blow to the rationale for maintaining large defense establishments. They seem to prefer the more cautious route of the CDE, in which agreement on confidence-building measures of evidently limited significance would place less strain on this rationale. Hence, the needed political impulse may not be forthcoming. In particular, the West Germans, who have most at stake on the Western side, have been ambivalent about the MBFR talks. At this juncture, the West German public would welcome any arms control agreement with the Soviet Union. But senior German officials and political leaders have been reluctant to contemplate reductions and other limitations restricted to the Federal Republic, the Benelux states, Poland, Czechoslovakia, and the GDR, and excluding both France and the western USSR, where many Soviet forces are deployed that would be used in the event of conflict with NATO. Many of these ground-force units are in a low state of readiness, suggesting the value of some future restraint on mobilization.

Although German leaders do see benefits in reducing military manpower to parity in MBFR, they also believe that reductions and control measures applied to the more limited MBFR area, as distinguished from the far larger area of application of CDE measures, could create a "special zone" prejudicial to West German interests, placing the FRG under restrictions not applicable to its European partners such as France and Great Britain, or to the Soviet Union. (The possible creation of a special zone comprising the two Germanies that might ultimately provide the basis for neutrality of the two German states was the ostensible reason for French refusal to participate in the MBFR negotiations and part of the motivation for French espousal of CDE covering a wider geographic area.) For these reasons, West German political opinion has been willing to contemplate restrictions on the size of out-of-garrison activities and reduction of armaments only in the larger CDE area rather than MBFR.

In sum, the outlook for the MBFR talks is not a very good one, despite their long-term potential for damping down the East-West confrontation. However, difficulties in the U.S.-Soviet nuclear talks could result in revival of interest in Vienna as a negotiation in which a relatively significant agreement could be achieved in a short time.

RELATING MBFR AND CDE

Aware of probable difficulties with France if they try to link CDE and MBFR, NATO governments have preferred to wait for one of these negotiations to produce a specific outcome before addressing the complex question of their future relationship. Even so, it may be useful to look into the future and to try to assess possibilities of integrating arms control in Europe by organizational means through combining these two negotiations in some way.

One hypothetical possibility is that in which both sets of negotiations, CDE and MBFR, culminate in a first agreement. In such an event, there would be a confusing overlap of similar measures—such as the obligation to report out-of-garrison activities in advance—undertaken for two different areas, on two different schedules, and in different degrees of stringency and commitment (because a CDE obligation is a declaration of intent whereas an MBFR agreement should culminate in a ratifiable treaty). One solution would be for the MBFR participants to consider as binding obligations those CDE measures that are applicable in the MBFR area and that in content go beyond commitments already assumed in MBFR. This would result in a single consistent set of obligations applying to the MBFR area and a second set of measures applying to the larger CDE area. A coordination center for MBFR could inform a CDE coordination center of details of implementation of measures taken under an MBFR agreement. Thus, one possible result of success in both negotiations would be two concentric circles of agreements, an inner MBFR area of more stringent measures and an outer CDE area of less binding obligations.

A second possible outcome is one in which one negotiation succeeds and the other does not. In present circumstances, the successful negotiation seems likely to be the CDE rather than MBFR. This outcome would certainly raise the question of the future of the MBFR negotiations and, with it, of the future prospects of achieving any East-West force reductions on a negotiated basis. In the event CDE has a first success while MBFR does not, it would be difficult to continue active negotiation in the MBFR forum considering the many years that MBFR has unsuccessfully dealt with troop reductions. In this event, negotiation could be suspended, maintaining the forum for future use and converting it for present purposes either to a NATO–Warsaw Pact crisis-control center or a center for theoretical discussion of strategies and military concepts of both sides. Another possible solution would be amalgamation of the two negotiations in a way that preserves the alliance-to-alliance format of MBFR for negotiating force reductions.

One possible construction might be to disband the MBFR talks in return for French agreement to establish a working group in the second phase of CDE, in which the participants would be the MBFR participants plus France. This augmented MBFR forum would deal with the area of greatest force concentration in Europe, Central Europe, and include in the reduction area to be covered by this working group the territory of France and the western USSR. Possibly, the Soviet Union might accept more stringent limitations on its own western territory if the territory of France were included in coverage of potential agreement. For its part, France might be willing to relax its objections to alliance-to-alliance negotiation if the negotiation took place in a forum subordinate to the CDE negotiation of which France was a major initiator. An alternative would be to establish a CDE Phase II working group to negotiate the reduction of forces (including French forces in the FRG) in the present MBFR reduction area, in which Soviet agreement to accept measures with a real bite is more plausible. Despite its refusal to participate in MBFR as it is now organized, France might agree to participate in such talks if they were embedded in the framework of a wider area (including France and the western Soviet Union) to which confidence-building measures and, ultimately, reductions might be applied.

CONTROLLING NUCLEAR WEAPONS IN EUROPE

The new INF forum agreed on in Geneva in January 1985 may be slow to bring specific results, and neither CDE nor MBFR as presently configured deals with nuclear armaments. If the views of France, which is a main initiator of CDE, prevail, CDE will be permanently precluded from dealing with nuclear weapons. Yet it is, of course, impossible to have serious arms control in Europe without bringing nuclear weapons under control.

The experience thus far has not been good. The effort in MBFR to negotiate withdrawal of U.S. tactical nuclear weapons from Europe against withdrawal of Soviet tanks did not succeed, perhaps because Western European NATO participants insisted on making U.S. nuclear withdrawals also conditional on Warsaw Pact agreement to massive additional manpower reductions. Although now resumed, the Geneva talks for reduction of intermediate-range nuclear armaments have broken down before. And, although the United States has (with NATO agreement) unilaterally withdrawn 1,000 nuclear warheads from Europe and plans to withdraw 1,400 further warheads, new Soviet and U.S. deployments have increased the number of nuclear launchers in Europe.

The issue of the nuclear balance in Europe has been dealt with by three separate approaches in three separate forums, which would have to be brought into some relationship with one another if there is to come about a more integrated view of arms control in Europe. These approaches are: (1) reduction and limitation of nuclear weapons, attempted in INF and MBFR; (2) geographical limitations of nuclear weapons deployment, that is, the concept of nuclear-free zones; and (3) possible East-West agreement on no first use of nuclear weapons.

An integrated approach would bring launchers of less than 1,000-kilometer range and their warheads under a regime of verified reductions, to be negotiated in the MBFR forum. Both sides appeared in the INF talks to contemplate a freeze on these weapons, but not reduction of them. NATO appears to be considering some further unilateral reduction of tactical warheads of nuclear artillery and other short-range weapons. This is a positive first step but will leave thousands still in position.

It seems probable that there will be continued support for a no-first-use commitment from the Soviet Union and other Warsaw Pact members, and from the parties of the opposition Left in Western Europe. Some of these parties may come to power in the next several years or may effectively urge existing governments to negotiate seriously on this topic. Because nuclear weapons would remain deployed on both sides, the main effects of a purely declaratory no-first-use commitment would be psychological, easing the concerns of some segments of Western public opinion. This is an inadequate basis for an East-West agreement. On the other hand, there seems no possibility that NATO will add sufficient conventional strength to convince political conservatives that NATO can afford to dispense with a flexible response strategy that entails possible first use. Therefore, if the topic remains politically active, one constructive way to handle it might be to link it to other stabilizing or arms control measures that would have some effect on the nuclear-force posture of the two sides. These measures could include zones of prohibited arms, wider on the Warsaw Pact than on the NATO side; taking forces off Quick Reaction Alert; and agreed reduction of nuclear warheads or of other armaments (such as tanks).

A NEW ORGANIZATIONAL FRAMEWORK

By combining CDE and MBFR and giving the new negotiation an expanded program, or by expanding the present MBFR talks, a comprehensive East-West set of negotiations might result, which would combine in a single integrated negotiating approach all the fields of possible arms control in Europe: confidence building, including constraints on force activities and deployments; reduction of possibility of surprise attack; and reduction of military manpower and armaments, including nuclear armaments. But unless altered drastically, the CDE framework is not very usable for such a purpose.

In the first place, France has refused to negotiate nuclear weapons in CDE. Second, a major, built-in positive element of the CDE concept—extension of geographic coverage to the western USSR— is at the same time a major weakness because the Soviet Union is unlikely to accept inspections and limitations on size of forces on its own territory unless the United States is prepared to subject its own home territory to parallel measures. Third, the thirty-five-country CDE forum appears to pose even more difficulties for force reductions negotiations than do the MBFR talks. It lacks the alliance-to-alliance, NATO–Warsaw Pact structure that is the strength of the MBFR talks: When we are discussing the risks of conflict and prospects for disarmament in Europe, we are discussing the NATO–Warsaw Pact confrontation, not the limited problems caused by the forces of the neutrals. Finally, the problem of agreeing on data remains a necessity for almost all forms of reductions. If unresolved in MBFR, it is unlikely to be solved in CDE. It is difficult to envisage a reduction concept that can be applied to thirty-five individual participants equally, and that would not accept in treaty form the cumulative numerical superiority of the Warsaw Pact countries over NATO states in most major armaments. The strength of the CDE framework is its continuity; but it appears that a major shortcoming of this format may be its inability to deal with reduction of forces or limitations on their size.

MBFR also has limitations as a forum for comprehensive negotiations. West German reluctance to negotiate reductions in armaments in an area that does not include France or the USSR will probably continue. The conflict between the West German view that there should be no armament reductions in the smaller MBFR area and the resistance of the Soviet Union to accepting measures applied to Soviet forces on its own territory probably means that there will be no agreement on armament reductions in either CDE or MBFR unless a change of basic views occurs on one side or the other. As suggested, the ideal solution would be to expand the MBFR reduction area by agreement to include the territory of France and of the western USSR. This would be an equitable trade, but it is uncertain whether France would agree.

Now that U.S.-Soviet agreement has been reached to establish three concurrent negotiations on space weapons, strategic nuclear weapons, and INF, it would be possible to deal with these shortcomings in another way, by adding a fourth area of negotiations—conventional and tactical nuclear forces in Europe and confidence-building measures—to the three already agreed. Including these topics in the coverage of such a unified negotiation would ensure that they receive the high-level attention they need to progress. With this approach, the United States and the Soviet Union would participate in all four such groups. European NATO and Warsaw Pact members would participate in at least the last two, negotiating along with the superpowers. In such a configuration, there could be direct participation in the intermediate and tactical nuclear reduction negotiations of those European countries on whose territory U.S. nuclear weapons are deployed. France would probably refuse to participate, at least at this stage, and would maintain its precondition of prior deep cuts by the superpowers. Interested European NATO members should also be given a role through membership in an advisory group, empowered to follow the negotiations on strategic weapons in detail and give advice on their strategy.

It is clear that the United States would be reluctant to take such actions. They would make U.S. strategic interests a topic subject to a common decision, and the difficulty of achieving consensus with allied European governments would further complicate the existing problem of reaching agreement on arms control positions within the administration. These would be serious obstacles. However, experience shows that the political costs of excluding the allies from arms control decisions would be still higher, as was demonstrated in the INF talks. These costs are likely to mount as long as the United States claims to extend nuclear protection to its allies but excludes them from direct participation in discussions with the Soviet Union that have a direct bearing on that protection and on their national survival. To have such decisions reached by a foreign government without sharing in them by direct participation in negotiation creates resentment and suspicion. This has already eroded the alliance and contributed significantly to the departure of France, and it has fractured domestic political consensus on NATO defense in other countries. There is probably no good solution for the fundamental question of how U.S. allies can participate in a U.S. decision on the possible use of nuclear weapons. But participation in arms control decisions and negotiations is a different and separable topic that needs to be addressed for the sake of alliance cohesion.

Long-term cohesion in the NATO alliance requires moving toward a principle whereby all nuclear weapons capable of hitting any part of the territory of either alliance are covered in East-West arms control negotiations, with direct European participation in those negotiations. The principle of shared risk of nuclear destruction requires some form of direct European participation in all East-West negotiations on arms control in Europe, including those on limiting nuclear weapons. If successful, such a comprehensive arms control approach could provide a unifying, sustaining concept for NATO for the coming decades, justifying NATO defense budgets under the objective of reduction and stabilization of the NATO–Warsaw Pact confrontation.

PROSPECTS FOR AN INTEGRATED REGIME

If East-West relations do not worsen significantly during the next four or five years, it will appear increasingly logical, desirable, even politically necessary to move forward in all areas of arms control in Europe. Nonetheless, the prospects for implementing an overall approach to arms control in Europe of the kind described here appear quite limited.

As regards its organization, a project of this kind would require firm and continuing pressure from at least one of the larger NATO governments. But on the Western side, the United States will remain reluctant to share control of its nuclear weapons and of its national security with its European allies. Despite the potential of the United States to provide creative leadership, continued divisions in U.S. leadership opinion over arms control will mean that this leadership will not be exercised with consistency and continuity. Strong French or West German leadership could be decisive. But France is unlikely to find acceptable an approach calling for strong alliance coordination. Despite its worries about the future posture of Germany, and despite its aspirations to leadership in Europe, France is not prepared to join in either the amalgamation of CDE and MBFR or the expansion of MBFR. France appears unable to abandon its preference for diplomatic autonomy to share sufficiently in the common fate of Europe to provide the needed forward impulse. In the Federal Republic of Germany, despite concerns about nuclear weapons, majority political opinion is unlikely to support actions either to obtain a credible conventional defense or to provide momentum in entering the fearsome territory of arms control agreements in which the Soviet Union is a major participant. For the foreseeable future, political opinion in the FRG will be sufficiently turbulent on defense and arms control issues to keep the entire West unsettled, without developing a sufficient internal consensus to make any given approach acceptable. Great Britain would be a conceivable source of leadership on European defense and arms control. But Tory governments have taken a very conservative position toward arms control in Europe during the 1970s and 1980s and, in negotiations like MBFR, have apparently conceived of their role as stiffening the NATO negotiating position against possible German or U.S. weakness.

These are important obstacles. But the main obstacle to success of any more ambitious approach to arms control in Europe is the near certainty that the Soviet Union will insist on keeping large forces in forward position in Eastern Europe. The failure of the Soviet Union and the Communist governments of Eastern Europe to make these governments self-sustaining without the presence of Soviet military forces is a major reason for this Soviet attitude. It is improbable that these Soviet forces will be used to attack Western Europe, but they will also not be moved back. Extremely powerful institutional interests will continue to support this essentially political motivation of the Soviet leadership; the main raison d'être of the Soviet ground forces and of their own claim on important allocation of Soviet resources is to deal with the Western military threat as the military leaders perceive and present it. This means, in practical terms, not only that the Soviet leadership will insist that large Soviet forces remain in Eastern Europe, but also that these forces will be well equipped, continuing the requirement for a balancing NATO force. For the foreseeable future, these factors establish narrow limitations to the possible scope of reductions of manpower and armament of Warsaw Pact forces to which the Soviet Union will be prepared to agree.

In short, it is unlikely that either side can muster the political will to carry through a broad approach to arms control in Europe. In the very long term, these obstacles to an integrated arms control approach may mean that gradual unilateral decline of forces on both sides is the only prospect for winding down the East-West military confrontation in Europe—unpredictable, frustrating, risky, and slow as such a process would be. In the interim, rather than being sustained by a grand design for arms control of compelling rationality and public appeal, the future of European arms control is more likely to consist of a patchwork of partial agreements and uncoordinated actions. In practical terms, Soviet reluctance to make major reductions in Soviet forces in Eastern Europe means that, for the foreseeable future, agreed reductions will be limited in scope and, consequently, that the main focus of arms control in Europe in coming years is likely to be in the confidence-building, crisis-control fields.

But even though a comprehensive integrated approach to arms control in Europe appears improbable for many years to come, achieving some larger measure of integration seems possible. For example, NATO defenses should be strengthened in ways that elicit broader public support and that have a parallel arms control content: possible adjustments, not radical reforms, of the present NATO defense posture in the Central Front. One possibility would be to establish a belt of static defense with weapons of limited range and with field fortifications along the West German eastern border with Czechoslovakia and East Germany. NATO armored and mechanized units would be grouped behind this defensive belt to deal with Soviet forces that may break through in the event of conflict. The combination of a defensive buffer zone, applying modern technology, with mobile armored forces like those NATO now possesses, could improve NATO chances of stopping a conventional attack without needing to resort to nuclear weapons. The belt of first contact would be manned by the same forces now responsible for the various sectors along the NATO border with Warsaw Pact forces and would therefore preserve the deterrent effect of having the FRG's NATO allies stationed forward, where they would make initial contact with Soviet forces, along with the West Germans, in the event of Soviet attack.

Such a defense concept could be valuable in itself and could be implemented unilaterally. The appropriate arms control complement would be a zone of reduced armaments on both sides of the West German border from which all tanks, self-propelled artillery, helicopters, and nuclear warheads and nuclear delivery systems would be banned. Such a negotiated zone would add to the stabilizing effects of unilateral action by NATO to establish a two-layer defense of its own. By pulling Soviet tank forces back fifty or a hundred kilometers, an additional period of warning would be achieved. Because the West would originally have taken the action on its own to improve its own defensive posture, there might not be much negotiating leverage to induce the Pact to follow suit in creating zones of limited armament, although the Soviet Union officially espouses the idea. The West may be able to find some additional inducement for the Soviets in the form of potential Western agreement to a no-first-use commitment.

As an additional condition for shelving its first-use doctrine, the West might press for an agreement to take the nuclear forces of both sides in Central Europe off Quick Reaction Alert and to reduce tactical nuclear armaments in Central Europe. Further possible conditions for Western acceptance of a no-first-use commitment might be withdrawal of a large number of Soviet tanks to the Soviet Union, as originally proposed in MBFR, or agreement in the MBFR talks on reducing military manpower to an equal level. Each of these possibilities would be worthwhile. Their negotiability may be questionable in the light of Soviet unwillingness to make large reductions in their forces in Central Europe, but the possibilities should be tested.

The appropriate form for negotiation on zones of reduced deployment is clearly MBFR. In the NATO–Warsaw Pact, alliance-to-alliance framework of MBFR it is possible to make a strong case for deeper zones on the Warsaw Pact side than the NATO side. First, in Central Europe—as defined in the MBFR talks—the territory of the Western portion, made up of the Federal Republic of Germany and the Benelux countries, is much smaller and narrower than the portion of Central Europe in the Warsaw Pact area, consisting of the territories of Czechoslovakia, the German Democratic Republic, and Poland. The ratio is 1:1.7. Second, the territory of the Soviet Union, the principal nuclear power of the Warsaw Pact, abuts directly on Central Europe, and the western USSR contains many tactical nuclear armaments capable of reaching targets in the NATO portion of Central Europe. The reverse cannot be said of tactical nuclear weapons located in the United States. U.S. air bases in the United Kingdom cannot make up for the ease with which the USSR can bring to bear in Central Europe its nuclear armaments stationed in the western USSR.

CONCLUSIONS

The limitations on the possible scope of East-West arms control agreements in Europe described in this analysis, arising from cross-purposes and lack of consensus in the West and from the probable unwillingness of the Soviet Union to make major reductions in its forces in Eastern Europe in the foreseeable future, argue against ambitious projects for far-reaching comprehensive arms control in Europe. But they do not preclude extremely valuable partial agreements. In the course of time, partial agreements could include: some reductions and limitations of manpower and armaments, both conventional and nuclear; constraints on deployment of manpower and armaments in certain areas; mutual inspection for verification and assurance against surprise attack; exchange of information; limitations on the size of out-of-garrison activity, prenotification of out-of-garrison activities, and presence of observers at them. Cumulatively, measures like these could make an important contribution to the stabilization of the East-West confrontation in Europe and would represent major gains in security for both sides. That East-West confrontation in Europe will continue and that the prospects for far-reaching arms control programs are slim are facts that make it even more worthwhile to seek agreement on such partial measures.

Even for a limited, partial program of this kind, it will be necessary for Western governments to carefully think through the relationship between CDE and MBFR and to expand the coverage of present negotiations. If Western political leaders, even those most skeptical about arms control, objectively weigh the pros and cons of arms control on a negotiated basis against the long-term problems of dealing with the decline in the West of public support for the East-West military confrontation in its present dimensions, it will be clear to them which alternative presents the greater danger for the West, and they will see the advantages of more serious, energetic efforts to achieve even partial agreements.

NOTES

1. Details on the present status of the CDE talks can be found in *Security for Europe* by James Goodby, the U.S. representative at the talks, in *NATO Review,* no. 3, June 1984, and in *The Conference on Disarmament in Europe,* Issue Brief Number IB84060, 1 June 1984, of the Library of Congress Congressional Reference Service.

2. Background on the MBFR talks is contained in my article "MBFR, from Apathy to Accord," in *International Security* 7 (Spring 1983):4.

4

ARMS CONTROL AND THE FEDERAL REPUBLIC OF GERMANY

WOLFRAM F. HANRIEDER

A consideration of the goals of nuclear-arms control must, in the first instance, recognize and accept the reality that arms control inevitably occurs in a political context. It is essential to realize that the intentions that drive arms control negotiations are not limited to the avoidance of war or the management of crisis situations but derive their larger meaning from political purposes—global, regional, and domestic. Arms control measures, even if they are intended to enhance the stability of the military balance, are the continuation of politics by other means.

For the United States and the Soviet Union, as well as for their respective allies, arms control has always had fundamental implications for the nature of East-West relations and for the shape of the global and European political order. The limits that define mutually acceptable arms control arrangements are the same limits that define political accommodation. When these limits have proven insufficiently flexible, neither political purpose nor arms control measures can be realized. To put it in a different way: Both arms control measures and political accommodation are functions of the existing balance of power. Neither the stabilization of the military balance nor the stabilization of the political balance can take place unless the competing parties can be confident that their power position remains unimpaired during or after the conclusion of arms control agreements or political arrangements.

This central axiom of arms control is supported by the historical record. Before the advent of strategic parity between the United States and the Soviet Union, neither superpower had a compelling interest in engaging in serious comprehensive arms control agreements: The United States, being superior, felt less urgency; and the Soviet Union, being inferior, was determined not to freeze permanently its position of relative weakness. It is also not coincidental that in the 1970s the tentative and modest steps toward arms control embodied in the first and second Strategic Arms Limitation Talks (SALT I and SALT II) were accompanied and sustained by an East-West agreement that it was in the common interest to stabilize and legitimize the European territorial and political status quo. Stabilization of the arms race and stabilization of the European status quo were the twin pillars on which the détente process of the early and middle 1970s rested.[1] Considerations of this nature also explain the reluctance of the first Reagan administration to engage in serious arms control negotiations. Washington showed little interest in reviving a process of détente, and it perceived the United States—accurately or not—as having fallen behind in the arms race with the Soviet Union. As George Ball has noted: "President Reagan's logic leads to a negation of arms control. If America is in the lead with respect to any new weapons, we should not give up that advantage by agreeing to outlaw or limit that system, but should instead push forcefully ahead. If, on the other hand, we are behind the Soviets in some new generation of weapons, we should reject any limitation until we have caught up and surpassed our adversary."[2]

It is precisely the connection between arms control and political purpose that makes it so difficult to establish precise criteria for the goals of arms control and to arrive at plausible definitions of what constitutes crisis stability. The technological and qualitative asymmetries that characterize weapons systems (which must somehow be cumulated to arrive at such additive notions as "rough equivalence" or "parity") are coupled with equally intractable asymmetries that derive from the different geopolitical positions of the two superpowers and their respective alliance systems. Add to that the immense difficulty of calibrating the political and diplomatic purposes that underlie issues of arms control, and it becomes apparent that attempts to quantify notions of stability are bound to be checked by the ambiguities and uncertainties inherent in the political process.[3]

NUCLEAR STABILITY AND ALLIANCE MANAGEMENT: DETERRENCE AND REASSURANCE

Throughout the thirty-five-year history of the North Atlantic Treaty Organization (NATO), the central military doctrine that governed all aspects of Western security policy was that of strategic deterrence, which served as the military-strategic implementation of the overarching U.S. political strategy of containment. Containment and deterrence were mutually reinforcing elements of U.S. global strategy that faced, at the divide of Europe, toward both East and West. The strategy was intended to check the Soviet Union at the same time that it established in Western Europe, and above all in the Federal Republic of Germany (FRG), the geopolitical base on which the U.S. Cold War effort could be securely emplaced. Just as containment embodied a dual component—one directed toward the Soviet Union, the other toward the FRG—so did deterrence. While one component of U.S. deterrence policy was aimed at the Soviet Union, threatening dire consequences in case of Soviet aggression, an equally important element was aimed at the United States' West European allies, reassuring them that their security interests were adequately accommodated by the first component. Together, the threat of punishing the opponent and the attending reassurance effect on the alliance made up the core of the transatlantic security partnership and underlined the determination of the United States to contain the Soviet Union and protect Western Europe.[4]

Over the decades, the deterring and the reassuring aspects of Western strategy (and the various doctrinal announcements that sought to serve both purposes) became much less complementary. The gradual weakening of U.S. strategic superiority vis-à-vis the Soviet Union brought with it the gradual weakening of West European confidence that the United States would risk national nuclear suicide for the sake of the alliance. As the Soviet Union began to reach nuclear parity with the United States and as the idea of extended deterrence became less convincing, the principles of deterrence and reassurance—on whose complementarity the common purpose and cohesion of the Atlantic security community ultimately rested—began to diverge.

This created a dilemma for which neither the United States nor the Europeans could be blamed, nor from which they could escape. Nuclear parity between the two superpowers led to conflicts of interest between the United States—which now needed to delay or otherwise qualify the use of nuclear weapons—and NATO partners at the forward line of defense, such as the FRG, who were prohibited from obtaining a national nuclear capability but could not accept a strategy that implied sustained conventional warfare at the expense of their territories and populations. The central dilemma of NATO during the last decade and a half could not be resolved: The United States, in seeking to limit the arms race and arrive at a stable nuclear balance, was compelled to deal with the Soviet Union on the basis of *parity,* as was reflected in the arrangements of the Strategic Arms Limitation Talks. At the same time, Washington could not convincingly guarantee the security of Western Europe except on the basis of an implied U.S. nuclear *superiority.* As a consequence, West Germany's initial misgivings about NATO's doctrine of flexible response were increased by the advent of U.S.-Soviet nuclear parity. The West Germans feared that deterrence would be weakened by the U.S. inclination to avoid or postpone nuclear intervention; that the idea of flexible response would add to the Warsaw Pact's geographical advantage with respect to deployment and resupply; and, most insidious, that the thinking behind flexible response implied the "divisibility" of deterrence, that Europe would become a battlefield while the United States remained a sanctuary.

All this brought into sharp focus the central paradox in the West European, and especially the West German, attitude toward their nuclear protector: They seemed equally afraid that the United States would use nuclear weapons or that it would not. The West Europeans feared, in equal measure, lack of U.S. circumspection and lack of U.S. resolve; they worried (especially during the Reagan administration) about the global confrontation with the Soviet Union that Washington seemed to favor, but they also feared the possibility of U.S. unilateralism and disengagement from Europe. Were it not for the fact that the Soviet Union, for its part, has been unable to fashion a sophisticated European policy—above all, in its apparent inability to define its security in terms other than military—the transatlantic connection would be even weaker than it already is. At any rate, it might be worthwhile for U.S. diplomacy to consider that "confidence-building measures" should be addressed to allies as well as to opponents; and that the widening gap between deterrence and reassurance can be narrowed only by an appropriately circumspect and measured U.S. diplomacy, coupled with a correspondingly plausible arms control strategy.

THE POLITICS OF ARMS CONTROL: THE FRG AND THE EUROPEAN POLITICAL ORDER

This is the context—as much political as it is military-strategic—in which the implications of arms control must be seen. And here again, the example of the Federal Republic of Germany is most instructive and justifies a short historical digression.

In the 1960s and 1970s, as the likelihood of war in Europe had diminished and as economic issues appeared more pressing than military ones, the Western powers could afford to use military terms to express what were at bottom political concerns. Security policies, strategic doctrines, and arms control proposals became saturated with purposes that were essentially political rather than military. The logic of power and the purposes of diplomacy were being expressed in the language of security and arms control. By the mid-1960s most of the major participants in the East-West dialogue on arms control had begun to use security policy to articulate and advance political objectives.

The political uses of strategic language and arms control proposals, and the general shift from military elements of power toward economic ones, were especially important to West Germany, for several reasons. First, because of its geography and history, from the beginning the FRG was a NATO member with special inhibitions, obligations, anxieties, and opportunities. Whatever problems plagued NATO because of waning U.S. nuclear superiority always were felt more keenly in Bonn than in other West European capitals. Because of legal, political, and psychological restrictions, the Federal Republic could not supplement its security connection with the United States by establishing a nuclear deterrent of its own—as had France and the United Kingdom—and the West Germans had relatively little influence in the nuclear management of the alliance on which their ultimate security depended. These considerations alone would have made it difficult for the West Germans to express political purposes in military-strategic language. But there were other inhibitions as well. Because of Germany's past, had the West Germans followed General Charles de Gaulle's example of couching political aspirations in terms of arms—the French *force de frappe* was, at bottom, as much a diplomatic as a military instrument—they would have been accused of being unreconstructed militarists. Especially sensitive was the question of any kind of German association with nuclear weapons: the German finger on the nuclear trigger. Whenever German policy touched upon nuclear matters—talks about a Franco-German nuclear consortium in the early 1960s, Germany's participation in the proposed multilateral nuclear NATO force, Bonn's footdragging on the non-proliferation treaty—anxiety levels rose in the West as well as in the East. The Germans had to speak softly indeed.

The case of West Germany is a special one for a second reason: The Federal Republic was one of the main political beneficiaries of the shift from military to economic-monetary expressions of power. Aside from the fact that West Germany's political and diplomatic leverage increased as its economic and monetary strength grew, economic and monetary "language" provided the West Germans with an excellent opportunity to translate political demands—which might still have been suspect because of Germany's past—into respectable economic demands. Although the Germans grumbled a good deal about the fact that they were always called upon to pay "subsidies" of one sort or another to one country or another, the shift from military to economic elements of power was highly advantageous to them. The transformation of economic power into political power, and the translation of political demands into economic terminology, compensated for the Germans' handicap of not being able to translate political demands into military-strategic language.

Above all perhaps, the FRG found it difficult to translate political purposes into the language of strategic doctrine because of its guarded view, in the 1950s and 1960s, of the ramifications of East-West arms control. The tortuous response of West Germany to the arms control proposals of the 1950s and 1960s stemmed in large measure from political misgivings over their repercussions on the issue of Germany's division. These various proposals, put forth by the East as well as by the West, played an important role in East-West diplomacy on the German question—that is, on the political configuration of the European order—and they were invariably freighted with implications for Bonn's Eastern policies that the West Germans found distasteful or outright unacceptable. The need to assess these implications distinguished the Federal Republic from other European NATO members. The FRG's relations with its Eastern neighbors were burdened by large unresolved issues, which stemmed from the refusal of successive Bonn governments to recognize the German Democratic Republic (GDR) and to accept as permanent, under international law, the Oder-Neisse borderline between Poland and the GDR. Because most arms control proposals for Europe implied recognition of the European status quo, and in some cases were specifically intended to serve that purpose, the West Germans responded to such proposals with caution ranging on suspicion, with hesitation ranging on procrastination and rejection.

The more accommodating attitude adopted by the Grand Coalition government (1966–1969) and especially by its successor, the Brandt government (1969–1974), stemmed from a realistic appraisal of the limits and opportunities of West German policy. The Brandt government, in particular, was sensitive to the fact that stalling European détente (because détente would bring with it a legitimization of the political status quo, that is, a legitimization of the East German state) would not serve West German political interests. Thus Bonn saw political advantages in backing détente and arms control measures, especially because the goals of West German *Ostpolitik* necessitated adopting a more conciliatory attitude toward the East. The Brandt government's *Ostpolitik* also became a complementary part of the FRG's security policies—not because *Ostpolitik* lessened the FRG's strategic dependence on the United States or its allegiance to NATO, but because Bonn's readiness to accept the territorial status quo tackled West German security problems at their political roots. In contrast to the 1950s and 1960s when Bonn's security policy conflicted sharply with its Eastern policy, *Ostpolitik* overcame these stark contradictions. By recognizing the territorial and political realities stemming from World War II, the West Germans meshed their security policy and their Eastern policy, developed a more constructive attitude toward arms control, and adjusted West German foreign policy to the dynamics of East-West détente.

THE EUROSTRATEGIC NUCLEAR BALANCE
AND THE EUROPEAN POLITICAL ORDER

The solid support given by both the Brandt and Schmidt governments to U.S.-Soviet strategic-arms control arrangements was, at bottom, predicated on the assumption that after reaching an East-West agreement on strategic intercontinental nuclear forces, the United States and the Soviet Union would then attempt to stabilize the eurostrategic intermediate-range nuclear balance on the Continent. This was less an issue during the years of the Brandt government, but became more pressing after the Soviet Union started deploying SS-20 missiles in the mid-1970s, augmenting its already existing capacity to reach any target in Western Europe with its nuclear arsenal.

In the 1970s, the Soviet Union not only achieved rough parity with the United States in strategic intercontinental capabilities, but gained a significant edge in eurostrategic nuclear capabilities. West German Chancellor Helmut Schmidt expressed concern over the growing eurostrategic nuclear imbalance in a much-noted speech in London in October 1977, in which he argued that nuclear parity, as institutionalized in the Strategic Arms Limitation Talks, had "neutralized" the nuclear capabilities of both sides and therefore magnified the significance of the disparities between East and West in tactical-nuclear and conventional weapons. (Even before Schmidt's speech, two NATO panels, one dealing with military aspects, the other with arms control aspects, had begun deliberations on the issues raised by the eurostrategic imbalance.) The Carter administration was not willing to complicate the ongoing SALT II negotiations with the question of eurostrategic weapons, nor were the president and his national security adviser, Zbigniew Brzezinski, convinced that the eurostrategic nuclear balance was a pressing issue. By the time the leaders of the United States, the FRG, France, and England met on Guadaloupe in January 1979, however, there was already some preliminary agreement to modernize NATO's intermediate-range nuclear weapons, which became coupled, at the meeting, with the idea to seek arms control measures at the same time. The December 1979 NATO "double-track" decision turned into a major political liability, however, inasmuch as the Europeans controlled only the deployment track of the decision while the arms control track was placed in the hands of U.S. and Soviet negotiators.

This must have appeared as an especially ironic consequence to Chancellor Schmidt, whose primary concern had all along been the political rather than the technical-military dimensions of the Soviet Union's extensive deployment of SS-20s. For the Schmidt government—and especially for the chancellor himself, who had become increasingly skeptical about the circumspection and consistency of U.S. diplomacy in general and that of the Carter administration in particular—the restoration of the eurostrategic *military* balance (either through the deployment of modernized NATO weapons or, preferably, the reduction of Soviet weapons) was the essential prerequisite for sustaining the European *political* balance. The West German chancellor feared that the Soviet Union would convert its eurostrategic nuclear advantage into political advantage, and he was worried that the United States might not resist such pressures firmly enough.

For the West German government the issue of whether eurostrategic nuclear parity would strengthen the U.S. strategic nuclear commitment to Western Europe or whether it would, on the contrary, enhance U.S. opportunities for limiting a nuclear war to Europe, was somewhat theoretical and academic. Helmut Schmidt prided himself on his pragmatism, and he considered the question of when and how a U.S. president might use nuclear weapons to be not only an unanswerable question but improperly posed: It postulated the most extreme, most incalculable, and most unlikely crisis situation. Schmidt was much more concerned with the more plausible if less dramatic possibility that the Soviet Union would derive considerable political leverage from the continuation of the eurostrategic imbalance.

Primarily for this reason the West German government sought a stabilization of the eurostrategic balance. But such stability failed to materialize when the Soviet Union continued to deploy SS-20s, making a codification of the eurostrategic balance increasingly difficult, and when President Carter's political fortunes in Washington fell so drastically that he could not obtain ratification of the SALT II treaty in the Senate and therefore could not proceed toward SALT III. Schmidt became stuck with the political liabilities of NATO's double-track decision, which he had urged in circumstances far different from the ones that prevailed at the end of the Carter and at the beginning of the Reagan administrations, and which he was obliged to defend in the face of mounting criticism in the FRG, above all in his own party.

Although Chancellor Schmidt was not terribly concerned about the issue of decoupling and the related question of what imponderables might sway the decision of a U.S. president to use nuclear weapons, a more tangible and immediate connection existed between the eurostrategic nuclear balance and West German politico-military interests. The restoration of the eurostrategic nuclear balance appeared essential to the credibility of the FRG's *conventional* deterrence posture. The connection between the eurostrategic force level and the U.S. global strategic deterrent seemed less important than the connection that existed "downward" to the conventional force level. For the Germans, rough parity on the eurostrategic nuclear level appeared as an essential prerequisite for maintaining the deterrence function of NATO's conventional forces.

This appeared to be in the German interest for several reasons. Chancellor Schmidt had a high regard for the fighting capabilities of the West German army, the Bundeswehr (he considered them second only to those of the Israeli army), and he believed that this assessment was shared by the Soviet Union. Restoring the eurostrategic nuclear balance would increase the importance of conventional capabilities and thus maximize the West German advantage—politically as well as for purposes of deterrence—provided by the efficiency of the Bundeswehr. The German disadvantage of not being a nuclear power would be compensated in some measure by underlining the military and political importance of the FRG's conventional capabilities, with the consequence that to some extent the West Germans could rely on their own deterrent forces rather than on those controlled by the White House.

Such considerations appeared especially pertinent; a number of influential Western analysts—fearing or anticipating the collapse of NATO under the weight of unresolved issues—called for a sweeping reorganization of NATO's organizational structure as well as for a reshaping of its strategy. In short, they called for a rethinking that would face squarely the implications for West European security of U.S.-Soviet nuclear parity. Among other suggestions, such as dropping NATO's long-standing option of first use of nuclear weapons,[5] some analysts argued for a return to the "basics" of European security— the defense of national territory. Such a policy would serve not only to stabilize the European political order but also would relegate nuclear weapons to a less obtrusive and more reassuring role. As Michael Howard put it: "The necessity for nuclear countermeasures should be fully and publicly explained, but they should be put in the context of the fundamental task which only non-nuclear forces can effectively carry out—*the defense of territory.* Nuclear deterrence needs to be subordinated to this primary task of territorial defense, and not vice versa."[6] The political implications of such a shift of emphasis toward territorial defense—especially if implemented with advanced conventional technology (for which bipartisan support existed in the FRG) and institutionalized through a European "diplomatic concert" on security measures—would be far-reaching. It would require the structural reform of NATO, enlarge the Europeans' share of defense burdens, and obtain for Western Europe—and the Federal Republic of Germany—a larger role in guiding events toward a new European political order.

THE REAGAN ADMINISTRATION'S CREDIBILITY GAP

A major burden was placed on U.S.–West German relations during the first Reagan administration because the president found it extremely difficult to persuade his West European allies that he was seriously committed to arms control. The Geneva talks on intermediate-range nuclear forces (INF) commenced ten months into the president's term and then, it seemed, only at the insistence of the U.S. Congress and of European leaders who were themselves pressed by expressions of public concern over the impending deployments of Pershing II and cruise missiles.[7] The Geneva talks on strategic-arms reduction (START) were started seventeen months after President Reagan took office and again only after extensive expressions of concern over the delay, in the United States as well as abroad. The administration placed known opponents of the SALT II treaty in key positions in its arms control agencies and negotiating teams and, even so, felt obliged to force the resignation of the director of the Arms Control and Disarmament Agency for being "overzealous." The president postponed indefinitely the negotiations on a comprehensive test ban treaty, arguing the need for more nuclear testing, even though these talks had been supported by every president since Dwight D. Eisenhower. Most disturbing of all, perhaps, the administration raised discussions about "protracted" nuclear war and U.S. determination to prevail in such a war; there was a nagging suspicion in Europe, fueled by injudicious U.S. statements, that Washington aimed for nuclear superiority over the Soviet Union and that the deployment of missiles capable of reaching the Soviet Union from Western Europe was one way of implementing that intention.[8]

The latter point appeared to be especially significant. The Reagan administration argued that the United States was inferior to the Soviet Union on the level of intercontinental strategic capabilities—an argument that the Schmidt government found implausible and that the Kohl government chose to ignore in public—and that this "window of vulnerability" should be closed as quickly and tightly as possible. This was to be accomplished, at great cost, by the continuing improvement of the three components of the U.S. strategic triad. The sea-based leg was to be improved by adding a new Trident nuclear-capable submarine each year and, above all, by increasing the accuracy of sea-based missiles by the late 1980s. The air-based leg was to be improved by the development of the B-1 bomber, as an interim solution until a multipurpose bomber with a strategic range and "stealth" technology could be deployed by the late 1980s or early 1990s, and by modifying the existing B-52 bomber fleet to accommodate air-launched cruise missiles.

The major problem was the intended modernization of the land-based leg of the triad. The technological and political infirmities of the MX program (both connected with the intractable problem of choosing a plausible basing mode) made it an unsatisfactory method for modernizing the Minuteman missile complex; and the proposed supplementary development of a large number of single-warhead Midgetman missiles with a mobile basing mode suggested a revamping of the U.S. negotiation position in the START negotiations. In any case, the modernization plans for any of the three legs of the triad could not, for technical reasons, be implemented until the late 1980s at the earliest.[9] This raised the question whether the Reagan administration intended the deployment in Western Europe of Pershing II and cruise missiles as a stop-gap measure—similar to the decision of the Eisenhower administration to deploy Thor and Jupiter missiles in the 1950s—until the perceived weaknesses in the U.S. intercontinental strategic arsenal could be redressed in the late 1980s.

All this called into question Washington's readiness to bargain away the deployment of Pershing IIs and cruise missiles in Western Europe; at the very least, would the United States fail to exploit the leverage that the deployment provided for the U.S. negotiating stance in Geneva? The administration's original position at the INF talks— the so-called zero option for eliminating all Soviet nuclear weapons aimed at Europe in exchange for U.S. agreement not to deploy Pershing II and cruise missiles—was clearly too unrealistic even for an opening position; and the U.S. refusal to face up to the implications of the

British and French strategic nuclear weapons (especially in light of their impending modernization) raised further questions about U.S. willingness to negotiate in earnest. Moreover, the Reagan administration's anti-Soviet rhetoric and its black-and-white view of the East-West contest called into question the substance as well as style of U.S. diplomacy. The failure of the Reagan administration to develop an attitude (not to speak of a policy) toward the Soviet Union that conveyed anything but confrontational hostility placed severe strains on the transatlantic alliance. Many West Europeans were determined to compensate for the lack of a constructive U.S. policy with one of their own, with the somewhat ironic result that they appeared more confident than their distant and secure transatlantic partner of being able to deal with the Soviet Union through diplomatic and political means.

THE FUTURE OF DETERRENCE
AND ARMS CONTROL

Most significantly perhaps, the euromissile controversy demonstrated that there was no longer agreement among the Western powers over the nature and intensity of the Soviet threat—one of the most fundamental issues that NATO needs to address and yet avoids. In part, no doubt, these differing assessments derived from the differing views provided by global and regional political perspectives: Washington sees itself challenged by Moscow everywhere and on everything (especially when the president views the global East-West contest as a zero-sum game between the United States and the Soviet Union); the Europeans take a more limited view of the Soviet threat. But the differing views of the Soviet Union cannot be explained by global and regional perspectives alone. It is difficult at times to avoid the impression that both nuclear superpowers seek to exploit their nuclear-strategic preponderance to compensate for diplomatic, political, and even economic infirmities, and to exploit their nuclear status for purposes of alliance management.

The militarization of diplomacy is especially important for the Federal Republic of Germany. NATO has contracted to an essentially bilateral security arrangement between the United States and the FRG; and the FRG is especially dependent on its transatlantic security partner. As a consequence, Washington's political use of military-strategic matters and arms control arrangements has had a profound effect on the limits and possibilities of West German diplomacy. Increased nuclear saturation of both German states has tied the

German governments even closer to their respective superpower protectors and to the respective views of the East-West conflict; it has emphasized the division of Europe and of Germany and has stood in the way of mapping more constructive ways to ease that division; and it has narrowed the range of East-West European diplomacy and supported the essentially conservative European policy pursued by both the United States and the Soviet Union. Should the West Germans have required further demonstration that arms control is connected with the shape of the European political order, it was provided for them when French President François Mitterrand, in a speech to the Bundestag in January 1983, supported the Kohl government in its determination to implement the NATO double-track decision while his fellow Socialists on the opposition benches were sitting on their hands amid the applause of the Christian Democrats. For all parties, domestic as well as international, the issue of the eurostrategic military balance was, at bottom, an issue of the European and East-West political balance and the future relationship between the two Germanys.

Such reflections lead inevitably to the question of what *political* considerations underlie the new arms control initiatives the second Reagan administration might be willing to entertain and negotiate. In an article in *Foreign Affairs*, Robert W. Tucker has suggested three ways in which, in principle, a faith in deterrence might be restored: (1) the restoration of U.S. strategic superiority; (2) U.S. withdrawal from "major postwar commitments," because it is *extended* deterrence that has lost its credibility and not the U.S. commitment to retaliate in response to a direct attack on the United States; and (3) the restoration of détente. As Tucker puts it: "The effort to regain strategic superiority, or some semblance thereof, and a policy of withdrawal are two radically different ways to attempt a restoration of faith in deterrence. Either way may be pursued largely independent of the will and desire of the Soviet Union. This is one of their undoubted attractions and is to be sharply contrasted with the third course, détente, which is evidently dependent on the cooperation of the Soviet government. The attraction of détente, on the other hand, is that it is easier to pursue than strategic superiority while less likely to result in the sacrifice that withdrawal probably entails."[10]

Clearly, each of those three options carries with it distinct and contradictory implications for the future arms control policies of the United States. Pursuing the first two would, in different ways, raise serious and perhaps debilitating obstacles to the future of East-West arms control, whereas the third would appear to hold the most promise. Looking at the record of the first Reagan administration, it appears that, in the absence of pursuing détente, Washington has pursued the alternatives of strategic superiority and, with modification, of withdrawal. The question should be raised whether the aim to regain strategic superiority and the option of withdrawal are in fact as "radically different" as Tucker suggested, or whether they are, to some extent, complementary. The withdrawal option, to be sure, is ambivalent and ambiguous. On the one hand, the Reagan administration has given little indication that it seeks a political and diplomatic turning-away from Europe toward a neo-isolationist global U.S. diplomacy, even though some administration spokesmen have flirted with a more Pacific-oriented U.S. policy.[11] On the other hand, the proposals incorporated in the president's Strategic Defense Initiative (SDI—the space-based missile defense colloquially known as "Star Wars") carry with them the implication that a "fortress America" is a feasible and desirable U.S. geopolitical option.

In this sense, the superiority option and the withdrawal option may not be as contradictory as they appear at first glance. In Western Europe, and especially in the Federal Republic of Germany, the implications of a space-based missile defense are in fact viewed with caution and a measure of suspicion. West German Defense Minister Manfred Wörner has expressed concern over a two-class system of security within NATO, in which the different vulnerabilities of the United States and Western Europe would be accentuated.[12] France and Britain must anticipate the essential obsolescence of their national nuclear arsenals if the Soviet Union, as is likely, develops a comprehensive missile defense system of its own.[13] There also emerges the troublesome question of whether the emplacement of functioning defensive missile systems might not lead to a tacit agreement between the nuclear superpowers to limit a nuclear exchange to Europe.[14]

The prospects of East-West arms control are more than ever connected with fundamental questions pertaining to the future arrangements of the European political order. With respect to the prospects of FRG-U.S. relations, it is almost certain that arms control issues—at all levels of the spectrum of deterrence—will retain a significance that goes far beyond their military-technical impact and extends into fundamental questions about the future of the transatlantic alliance. West German attitudes, among decision makers as well as among the public at large, are and will continue to be formed by the issue of arms control; that issue will reverberate and extend into adjacent issues of West German–U.S. relations and affect them for years to come.

NOTES

1. For a fuller discussion of this connection, see Wolfram F. Hanrieder, *Fragmente der Macht: Die Aussenpolitik der Bundesrepublik* (Munich: Piper, 1981), and Helga Haftendorn, *Sicherheit und Entspannung* (Baden-Baden: Nomos, 1983).

2. George W. Ball, "White House Roulette," *New York Review of Books,* November 8, 1984, p. 6.

3. See, for example, the unconvincing and somewhat apologetic attempts made at measurement by the contributors to Daniel Frei, ed., *Definitions and Measurements of Détente: East and West Perspectives* (Cambridge, Mass.: Oelgeschlager, Gunn & Hain, 1981), passim. Consider also the biting comments by George W. Ball about the academic "priesthood" that has sought to impose "logic on inherently irrational nuclear conflict." Ball argues ("White House Roulette," p. 5) that the decisions of politicians and military commanders in crisis situations are shaped by a large variety of irrational and incalculable factors. "Since these factors are not susceptible to quantitative appraisal the methodologies employed by the priesthood limit the raw material of their speculations to an assessment of the physical capacities of weapons, on which they erect hypothetical 'scenarios.' Although some of those constructions can be rationalized within the closed logic of the experts, their inability to factor in political probabilities has unrealistically distorted not only the design of weapons systems but also arms control negotiations, often creating ectoplasmic bogymen." In a similar vein, George Kennan has repeatedly suggested that it is precisely in circumstances in which a rough equilibrium of *capabilities* prevails between adversaries that we must concern ourselves more with political *intentions.*

4. See Michael Howard, "Reassurance and Deterrence: Western Defense in the 1980s," *Foreign Affairs,* Winter 1982-1983.

5. See McGeorge Bundy, George F. Kennan, Robert S. McNamara, and Gerard Smith, "Nuclear Weapons and the Atlantic Alliance," *Foreign Affairs,* Spring 1982. For a German response to Bundy et al., see Karl Kaiser, Georg Leber, Alois Mertes, and Franz-Joseph Schulze, "Nuclear Weapons and the Preservation of Peace," *Foreign Affairs,* Summer 1982.

6. Howard, "Reassurrance and Deterrence," p. 354; see also Hedley Bull, "European Self-Reliance and the Reform of NATO," *Foreign Affairs,* Spring 1983.

7. In a speech delivered in Moscow in June 1984, Horst Teltschik, senior adviser on security and foreign affairs to Chancellor Kohl, made the following claim for the West European and especially the West German role in pushing for arms control measures: "We Europeans do not overestimate our role. Experience has shown that Moscow and Washington can very quickly resume talks if it suits their interests to do so. But we can help because we have a rich common history with the Soviet Union, as with Poland, Czechoslovakia, Hungary, Rumania and Bulgaria. We have a great common cultural heritage, we enjoy close economic relations and are bound by a common destiny."

Teltschik went on to say, "We have already achieved much in this way: in the development of East-West trade, in the successful conclusion to the CSCE follow-up conference in Madrid, which led to the opening of the Stockholm conference on Confidence and Security-Building Measures in Europe. *The last substantial proposals from the USA at the INF negotiations in Geneva, at the MBFR negotiations in Vienna and at the Geneva negotiations on the worldwide ban of chemical weapons were largely brought about by the Federal Government and other European partners who exercised a major influence on them* (emphasis supplied)." *Konrad-Adenauer-Stiftung* publication, p. 16.

8. See Strobe Talbott, *Deadly Gambits: The Reagan Administration and the Stalemate in Nuclear Arms Control* (New York: Alfred A. Knopf, 1984).

9. Projected initial operational capability (IOC) for the weapons systems involved in the U.S. strategic force modernization program, assuming full funding, are as follows:

- Advanced B-1B—IOC September 1986; full capacity June 1988
- Stealth Bomber—IOC early 1990s
- Midgetman—IOC 1989 in some modes
- Trident II (D-5) with Mark 500 Evader warhead—IOC FY 1989

See *Aviation Week and Space Technology,* 14 March 1983, pp. 23–31.

10. Robert W. Tucker, "The Nuclear Debate," *Foreign Affairs,* Fall 1984.

11. For a fuller exploration of this orientation, see Eberhard Rein, "Die pazifische Herausforderung—Gefahren und Chancen für Europa," *Europa-Archiv* 39, Heft 4, 1984, pp. 101–110; Wolfram F. Hanrieder, "Grundprobleme der deutsch-amerikanischen Beziehungen," *Merkur,* Heft 5, 1983, pp. 518–530.

12. Manfred Wörner, cited in *Süddeutsche Zeitung,* 29 April 1984. See also Egon Bahr, in *Vorwärts,* 31 March 1983; and David Yost, "Die Sorgen der Europäer gegenüber den amerikanischen Plänen für eine Raketenabwehr," *Europa-Archiv* 39, Heft 4, 1984, pp. 432 ff.

13. See *Europa-Archiv* 38, Heft 22, 1983, pp. 640–644; ibid. 39, Heft 7, 1984, pp. 195–200. Also see Western European Union, *WEU Document 976,* "The Military Use of Space," 15 May 1984.

14. See the testimony of Gerhard Wettig before the Defense Committee of the German Bundestag, in *heute im bundestag,* 12 June 1983.

5

ASSURED STRATEGIC STUPIDITY: THE QUEST FOR BALLISTIC MISSILE DEFENSE

RICHARD NED LEBOW

I call upon the scientific community who gave us nuclear weapons to turn their great talents to the cause of mankind and world peace: to give us the means of rendering these nuclear weapons impotent and obsolete.
—President Ronald Reagan, 23 March 1983

In his now famous "Star Wars" speech of March 1983, President Reagan unveiled his Strategic Defense Initiative (SDI), a "comprehensive and intensive effort" with the "ultimate goal of eliminating the threat posed by strategic nuclear missiles." Reagan's vision of SDI relies upon as-yet-undeveloped space weapons that, as Secretary of Defense Caspar Weinberger told "Meet the Press," would provide a "thoroughly reliable and total" defense.[1] The scientific community has on the whole scoffed at such claims.[2] This chapter explores the controversy that surrounds the president's $26 billion initiative; it evaluates the prospects for a successful ballistic missile defense (BMD) and the political and strategic implications of a national effort to secure one.[3]

The president's speech may have focused the public's attention on space weapons and ballistic missile defense, but it certainly did not mark the beginning of U.S. military efforts in space. For some years, intensive research has been under way to develop the technologies necessary for both antisatellite (ASAT) weapons and BMD. In June

1984, the United States conducted a successful test of an ASAT, the army's Homing Overlay Experiment (HOE). In 1985, the air force is scheduled to test its ASAT, a two-stage rocket launched from an F-15.[4]

ASATs and BMD represent different but nevertheless related aspects of the militarization of space. ASATs are designed to destroy enemy satellites used for early warning, surveillance, communications, and battle management. BMD would be used to destroy enemy ballistic missiles and thereby protect one's own homeland from nuclear destruction. Both weapons embody common technology; ASATs in fact represent an important stepping-stone toward BMD. These weapons also perform related missions, as ASATs could be used in conjunction with BMD to reduce the scale and effectiveness of an adversary's missile strike.[5]

ASATs are the more feasible of the two weapon systems. Each superpower already possesses some kind of ASAT and, in the absence of an arms control agreement, can be expected to develop considerably more advanced and capable weapons in the course of the next decade. BMD, by contrast, is more visionary in both its promise and its technology. It holds out the prospect of removing the threat of nuclear annihilation that has hung over our heads since the dawn of the atomic age. But, as we shall see, it is based on technologies that do not yet exist. Even if they could be perfected, BMD, contrary to the president's expectations, would be more likely to undermine than augment U.S. security.

BALLISTIC MISSILE DEFENSE

For those who have followed the evolution of the arms race, President Reagan's Strategic Defense Initiative has a sense of déjà vu about it. The late 1960s also witnessed a preoccupation with strategic defense and, with it, strong pressure from many quarters to build an antiballistic missile (ABM) defense. For Lyndon Johnson, president at the time, the decisive question was whether the proposed defense would work against Soviet ICBMs (intercontinental ballistic missiles). Would it destroy *all* incoming warheads? It was not enough, he insisted, to destroy only half or two-thirds of these warheads, as it took only one to destroy Washington. The unanimous judgment of Johnson's chief science adviser, the three previous science advisers, the Joint Chiefs of Staff, and the last three directors of research and engineering in the Pentagon was no.[6]

A few years later, the Soviet Union also became disenchanted with the prospects of ballistic missile defense. Mutual recognition of the technical futility of BMD paved the way for arms control talks, which led in 1972 to the Strategic Arms Limitation Talks (SALT) I and Anti-Ballistic Missile (ABM) treaties.[7] Research on BMD has nevertheless continued in the decade since the ABM Treaty and its 1974 Protocol in spite of what the distinguished British scientist, Solly Zuckerman, calls "the irrefutable logic of the technical argument that no BMD system could ever be devised that would provide either side with a guarantee that it could escape disaster in a nuclear exchange."[8] Is there any reason to suppose that the recent technological advances have in any way rendered this judgment obsolete?

The Life History of a Missile

To evaluate the feasibility of a ballistic missile defense it is first necessary to understand the several phases an ICBM passes through from launch to impact. Each of these phases poses different kinds of opportunities and problems for the defense. For this reason, most of the defensive systems now under discussion would operate during only one of the three phases of a missile's life. A layered defense, one that attacked ICBMs throughout their trajectory, would accordingly require several different weapon systems, each specific to a phase.

Boost Phase. The flight of an ICBM begins with its silo cover sliding back or popping open. The missile usually is then ejected by hot gases, and once outside the silo its first-stage booster ignites. When the first-stage booster burns out it falls away and the second stage takes over. This process then repeats itself, as most ICBMs have three booster stages. The portion of the journey from the silo to the point at which the last stage stops burning is known as the boost phase. For the MX missile, typical of ICBMs with a short boost phase, this would be after 180 seconds at an altitude of 150 miles.

Boost phase is the critical stage for missile defense for four distinct and equally important reasons. First, the boost phase confronts the defender with the smallest number of targets to be destroyed. When the boost phase ends, the remaining stage, known as the MIRV (multiple independently targetable reentry vehicle) bus, releases a number of warheads, anywhere from three to fourteen on missiles now operational. These travel along somewhat different paths toward separate targets, along with any decoys designed to complicate and confuse the defense. Second, the booster flame makes the ICBM a readily identifiable target. It emits a vast amount of infrared radiation that can be detected easily and almost instantly by satellite sensors tens of thousands of miles distant. This infrared signature can give the defender an accurate fix on the missile's location, an essential first step toward destroying it. When the boost phase ends, target acquisition becomes much more difficult. The defender must search for the very weak infrared signal emitted by warheads and decoys, or the defender must illuminate the warheads with radars or lasers and detect the reflection of the microwaves or laser light from them.

Third, a boost-stage missile constitutes a much larger and more vulnerable target than the warheads it subsequently releases. The MX missile, for example, is 21.6 meters (71 feet) long and 233 centimeters (92 inches) wide. Its ten warheads themselves are only 175 centimeters (68.9 inches) long and 53.3 centimeters (21.8 inches) wide at the base.[9] The warheads are also hardened to protect them against the rigors of reentry. The skin of the missile is, by comparison, relatively fragile. Finally, the problems associated with mid-course and terminal interception are so enormous that they are feasible only as adjuncts to a highly effective boost-stage defense. Administration officials themselves have cited the figure of 90 percent as the minimum acceptable efficiency of the boost-stage part of a layered defense.[10]

Mid-course. Once the MIRV bus has released all its warheads and decoys, the missile is said to enter its mid-course. In addition to warheads, a modern ICBM can fractionate into more than one hundred decoys, quantities of chaff, and clouds of emitting aerosols—no longer one object in space but a veritable swarm. By mid-course, a thousand missiles could present the defense with more than a hundred thousand potential targets, all of them concealed within clouds of debris. As space is a near vacuum, these objects, regardless of their size or shape, would proceed along ballistic trajectories, making it impossible with even the most precise tracking to discriminate warheads from decoys and chaff. The defender would have to destroy or somehow interfere with the entire swarm in order to identify the heavier warheads. Because target acquisition is so difficult, mid-course interception is generally recognized as the most daunting possible phase of missile defense.

Reentry. The final phase of the ICBM's journey begins when the objects it has released reenter the atmosphere. Defense becomes theoretically more feasible again because it is now possible to distinguish warheads from decoys and chaff. The warheads are carried by specially shaped and protected reentry vehicles (RVs) whereas the decoys and chaff burn up or slow down more rapidly when exposed to the friction of the atmosphere. Terminal defenses that destroy a high percentage of incoming warheads could conceivably protect discrete hardened targets such as missile silos. It is more reasonable to expect that they could make an attack more expensive by compelling an adversary to expend two, three, or many times the number of warheads to destroy a given set of targets. Terminal defenses could not protect "soft targets" like cities because warheads can be "salvage fused," set to detonate prior to interception.[11] A 50-megaton warhead so fused and exploding at an altitude of 30 kilometers would set fires and do major damage over more than 1,600 square kilometers.[12]

Antiballistic Missile Weapons

Three fundamental decisions must be made by a would-be defender: at which phase (or phases) to intercept the adversary's ICBMs, the type (or types) of weapons with which to do this, and whether to deploy them on the ground or in space. It is readily apparent that any effective defense must concentrate on the boost phase. This could, however, be part of a layered defense that attempted to destroy in mid-course and reentry those warheads that survived boost phase. The choice of where to deploy BMD weapons is also a relatively straightforward one. Neither Soviet missile silos nor the missiles themselves during their boost phase are in line of sight from the United States or allied territory. Weapons designed to be used during the boost phase would accordingly have to be deployed in space.

These weapons could be permanently in orbit or be sent into space in response to satellite warning of attack. Weapons in orbit—so-called orbiting battle stations—can be placed in low orbits just outside the atmosphere at about 1,000 kilometers (600 miles) or in geostationary orbits some 35,200 kilometers (22,000 miles) out, where they appear to remain poised over one spot on the ground because their rotation is precisely in step with that of the earth. Either option encounters formidable difficulties.

Low orbits have the advantage of being relatively close to the adversary's missile silos. However, the laws of motion require a satellite in low orbit to circle the earth every ninety minutes. As the earth itself also revolves, the satellite is above a different point on the ground after each circuit. Because of this, a low-orbit battle station would be within range of an adversary's missile silos only once or twice a day. To provide constant and sufficient coverage of Soviet missile silos, large numbers of battle stations would have to be put into orbit. According to the Union of Concerned Scientists, a minimum of 300 battle stations would be needed, and this assuming that all of them worked perfectly. They estimate that it would cost at least $13 billion just to lift these battle stations and their fuel into orbit![13]

Geostationary battle stations would always be above their targets but forty times further away from them than would be stations in low orbits. The tremendous distance between satellite and target severely curtails the kinds of weapons that might be used. Any of those that are theoretically possible are entirely visionary given today's technology. The cost of lofting payloads into geostationary orbits is also much higher than the cost of putting them in low orbits, so that a constellation of geostationary battle stations—if they ever became feasible—would cost even more than their low-orbit counterparts, even though fewer of them would be necessary.[14]

Another alternative is to "pop up" battle stations into space when an attack is detected. They would fire their weapons after having reached sufficient altitude to be in line of sight with the Soviet missiles. The size and shape of the earth would make it necessary for an interceptor fired from Alaska, the part of the United States closest to Soviet missile silos, to climb to an altitude of 2,000 miles before the missile fields of Siberia and the southern USSR became visible. By then, the target missiles would have passed through their vulnerable boost stage. The only way of overcoming this problem would be to find launch sites closer to the missile fields. Polaris or Trident submarines stationed in the Indian Ocean would be the most plausible choice but would require a vast new fleet of missile-launching submarines; the existing force would be insufficient for the task and in any case already has important strategic missions to perform. The navy would also probably need a fleet of attack submarines and surface vessels to protect the new SLBMs (submarine-launched ballistic missiles).

Any of the basing modes we have discussed would of necessity entail attacks against missiles at great or even enormous distances. It is therefore essential to employ weapons that can fire their projectiles at tremendous speeds. Laser beams, which move at the speed of light (186,000 miles per second) would be ideal, as would be beams of atoms or electrons that travel almost as fast. The trick is to make such directed energy weapons intense enough to cause the required damage at such large distances.

A laser is a device that emits a beam of light composed of nearly parallel rays. Three types of lasers are currently under consideration by the Department of Defense as anti-ICBM weapons: chemical lasers that emit infrared light, excimer lasers that emit ultraviolet light, and a laser pumped by x-rays emitted by a nuclear explosion.[15] Chemical and excimer lasers would be directed against a target by a mirror or set of mirrors. The laser itself could remain on the ground, but its mirrors must be in space in order to direct the beam at target ICBMs in their boost phases. This basing mode would rely on "active optics" to overcome the scattering of directed light beams caused by atmospheric turbulence. To cope with bad weather, especially energy absorbing cloud cover, ground-based lasers would have to be widely distributed in order to have a sufficient number of them free of cloud cover at any given time.

The principal difficulty with laser weapons is that the beams cannot retain their concentrated focus over any distance. In response to immutable physical laws, a laser beam spreads in proportion to the light's wavelength and the distance from the focusing mirror.[16] A 1-meter mirror focusing light of a 1-micron wavelength at a range of 1,000 kilometers (600 miles) would make a spot at least 1.3 meters (51 inches) in diameter, larger than the mirror itself. As the target became more distant, the beam would lose its effectiveness rapidly as it spread, in proportion to the *square* of the distance, even if the aim were perfect.

At the present time, chemical lasers are the most powerful ones yet devised, using the reaction between hydrogen and fluorine as an energy source. The wavelength of the light they produce is 2.7 microns, making them suitable only for low-orbiting battle stations. The Fletcher Commission, set up by the president to explore the potential of BMD, thinks that a two-megawatt laser could be developed by 1987.[17] According to the Fletcher Commission, a laser must deposit at least 180 megajoules of energy on the skin of a booster to make it ripple or rupture and thereby put it out of action. This could be accomplished by a laser that put out twenty-five megawatts of power and was capable of dwelling on the same spot on the booster for a full seven seconds. This assumes that its focusing mirror is geometrically perfect, as any imperfection will widen the laser beam and correspondingly reduce the energy it deposits per unit area. But such imperfections would almost certainly exist, as they cannot now be eliminated even under the best laboratory conditions.

A twenty-five-megawatt laser, far beyond anything we now possess, is theoretically possible to build but would almost certainly be enormous in size. Because of the physical laws governing the motion of low-orbiting satellites, a minimum of 300 lasers—or at least their mirrors—would have to be put into orbit. This would be an enormously expensive exercise. It would also require a tracking and focusing mechanism precise enough to keep the laser beam focused on the same spot on the missile over a distance of 1,000 kilometers for the number of seconds necessary to damage it.

The difficulties of exploiting chemical laser beams for ASAT weapons have kindled interest in x-ray lasers. X-rays have very short wavelengths (10^{-3} to 10^{-4} microns) and, as they are a form of light, travel as rapidly as other lasers. The great advantage of the x-ray laser is that it is the lightest kind of directed energy weapon. This is so because it exploits, quite inefficiently, the tremendous energy of a nuclear explosion. Although x-ray lasers thus constitute the most likely candidate for a pop-up defense against boosters, they have special drawbacks of their own.' They are rapidly absorbed by the atmosphere and would be useless against short-boost ICBMs whose boosters burned out in the atmosphere. Because of their exceedingly short wavelength they cannot be reflected by mirrors. Consequently, they cannot be focused in beams as parallel as those of chemical lasers and for that reason could not effectively be deployed on geostationary battle stations. The x-ray source must be put in a low orbit or popped up.

Particle-beam weapons, another alternative that is being explored, exploit the technology of particle accelerators to direct a beam of electrically charged particles, such as electrons or protons, toward a target. For particle beams to be effective as weapons, scientists would somehow have to overcome the principle drawback associated with particle-beam propagation: Charged particles follow a curved path in the magnetic field of the earth and therefore cannot be aimed accurately. One possible solution would be to employ neutral particle beams, which follow a straight path. The difficulty here would be to construct a device light enough to loft into orbit; neutral beam particle accelerators are notoriously heavy devices, a reasonably powerful one weighing upward of 500 tons. Even assuming some kind of miniature accelerator could be perfected, missile interception would have to take place above the atmosphere, as neutral atoms are broken up into electrons and electrically charged ions when they collide with air molecules. The resulting charged beam would fan out and be bent by the earth's magnetic field; it would be useless as a weapon.

The final weapon to consider is the kill vehicle, which attempts to intercept missiles, usually with small homing projectiles that can destroy a booster by impact. A homing projectile carries infrared telescopes, which enable it to sight a booster flame, a well as a computer and set of thrusters that allow it to correct its course and zero in on the target. All kill vehicles are slow in comparison to directed-energy weapons—at least ten thousand times slower—but they have several advantages over them. They do not require entirely novel technology, as they are based on well-understood scientific and engineering principles. Because one projectile can destroy a booster upon impact, kill vehicles do not require the sophisticated tracking that laser weapons need to dwell on a precise spot on a booster for several seconds. They also obviate the need for mirrors in space, which are extremely vulnerable.

The Defense Department is attempting to develop an orbital electromagnetic railgun that will fire kinetic energy rounds over 1,000 kilometers (600 miles) at a rate of 60 shots/second.[18] The aim is to accelerate these projectiles to velocities in excess of 100 kilometers (62 miles)/second. Such velocities would represent a notable accomplishment, as the highest velocity now attainable by railguns in earth-based laboratories is only 8.6 kilometers (5.3 miles)/second—much too slow to intercept boosters or warheads. Experimental railguns currently fire very small pieces of Lexan as projectiles. Lexan cannot be accelerated beyond 4.5 kilometers (2.8 miles)/second within the atmosphere without burning up, making it useless against ICBM boosters. Projectiles operating at higher speeds would require active cooling, perhaps by transpiration, that is, by boiling off fluid stored inside. In addition, such a weapon system would require a remarkably precise aiming mechanism, as the projectiles would be much too small to contain any kind of homing device. An enormous number of them would be required because one railgun can only attack one booster.[19]

Countermeasures

Most of the weapons we have discussed would be designed to intercept missiles in their boost stage. All of them require as-yet-undeveloped technologies to proceed beyond the stage of an interesting idea. By contrast, the variety of countermeasures that could be used to foil them exploits existing technologies that are easier and cheaper to implement.

Boost-phase interception schemes are vulnerable to a number of generic countermeasures, measures that do not depend on the specific characteristics of the weapons in question. Three kinds of counter-measures are worthy of consideration. First, battle stations in space would be far more vulnerable to attack than the ICBMs they are supposed to destroy. Battle stations would have to spend months in known or predictable orbits, making them much easier to target than boosters, which traverse much less predictable paths in several minutes or less. Indeed, few targets would be as easy to destroy as a ten-meter mirror that must retain its perfect shape and reflectivity to focus laser beams against target ICBMs. An "anti-BMD" satellite, circling the earth in the opposite direction from the target mirror or battle station, could release a swarm of steel pellets into its path. A one-ounce pellet colliding with its target at ten miles per second, its likely impact velocity, could penetrate six inches of steel. Battle stations could not be protected against such a weapon. Space mines could also be used to attack a large number of battle stations at the same time; the mines could be parked near their targets and detonated by remote control just prior to an ICBM attack. If and when ASATs are developed that are capable of destroying almost simultaneously large numbers of space platforms—the very technology on which so many proposed BMDs depend—battle stations will become sitting ducks.

Boost-phase interception also suffers from the need to intercept anything that behaves like an ICBM booster; BMDs cannot wait until the boost phase is over to discriminate real weapons from fakes. If a BMD system was deployed, and the ABM and SALT II treaties became dead letters, there would no longer be limits on ICBM deployments or concealment measures. The Soviets could defeat the BMD by swamping it. As Richard DeLauer, the Reagan administration's under secretary of defense for research and engineering, admitted, "With unconstrained proliferation, no defensive system will work."[20] The cheapest way to overwhelm a BMD would be to deploy fake ICBMs, boosters lacking costly guidance packages and warheads. An attack could begin by launching a large number of these fakes with exactly the same observable characteristics as their real counterparts. The defender would therefore have to attack them. After the laser-fueled, pop-up, or kill-vehicle weapons used to intercept these counterfeit ICBMs became depleted, the real attack could commence.

An even easier method for defeating most boost-phase BMDs would be to shorten the duration of that phase. An MX missile's rockets burn for a total of 180 seconds, during which time it is most vulnerable to attack. An MX, or its Soviet counterpart, could be reengineered to have a much shorter boost phase, say 50 seconds, and to fly in a depressed trajectory largely or even entirely within the protection of the atmosphere.[21] This would rule out any possibility of using x-ray and particle-beam weapons against it, as they cannot successfully penetrate the atmosphere. Such a move would also defeat most pop-up schemes by depriving them of the time they need to get aloft and in position to fire. A depressed trajectory requires no special technology, only the funds to develop faster-burning and structurally sturdier boosters. The Fletcher Commission reported that it would be possible to develop a booster that would burn out after only 40 seconds at which point the ICBM would have attained an altitude of only fifty miles.

A depressed trajectory would not only make the attacker's ICBMs impervious to x-ray and particle-beam weapons but would also significantly reduce the time available to lasers to dwell on the missile's skin. More powerful lasers would be required, which in turn could increase by severalfold the weight of the BMD weapons that would have to be lofted into space. Lasers could also be defeated by giving ICBMs highly reflective surfaces or by rotating them while in flight so that the laser, even if focused properly, scribed an arc instead of depositing its energy on the same spot on the missile's skin. Once again, more powerful lasers would be needed. Skirts could be rigged around the booster's nozzles to hide its flame, greatly complicating the task of locating and tracking it, or pollutants added to the propellant that would burn with great intensity at unpredictable intervals in order to confuse target acquisition sensors.

Mid-course interception is subject to even more countermeasures, most of them designed to hinder target acquisition. Target acquisition is more difficult in mid-course than in boost phase in any case because the objects to be tracked are both cooler and much more numerous. Tracking can best be accomplished by detecting visible or infrared light emitted or reflected by the target; optical sensors use mirror telescopes to pass electrical signals on to computers for processing and battle management. These sensors can be defeated by swamping, masking, signature suppression, or jamming. The simplest technique is to surround warheads with a cloud of decoys, chaff, and aerosols, confronting the defender with the all but impossible task of tracking and destroying two hundred thousand separate objects. Some of these decoys could be active, with radar transponders that send back fake echoes simulating the echoes of warheads. The passive decoys could be shaped to return especially strong optical or radar reflections. Warheads could be enclosed in balloons with thin metal-coated layers, so that all balloons—decoys as well as those containing warheads—would have the same visual appearance and radar signature. In addition, both RVs and decoys could be given the capability to maneuver, frustrating passive tracking schemes that depend on the tracked objects following a ballistic trajectory. Many of these countermeasures would also be applicable to a terminal defense system.

An attacker could also invest in alternative kinds of delivery systems that would entirely circumvent a ballistic missile defense. In addition to cruise missiles and ICBMs with depressed trajectories, unconventional solutions are also conceivable. For example, nuclear weapons could be "pre-delivered" by importing them clandestinely onto enemy territory;[22] the increasing miniaturization of nuclear warheads has made such a venture much more feasible than was ever the case in the past. Such responses would not only bypass a BMD but would also reduce the warning time of attack.

Our analysis makes clear that total ballistic missile defense—the protection of U.S. society against the full weight of a Soviet nuclear attack—is unattainable if the Soviet Union exploits the many vulnerabilities intrinsic to all the schemes that have thus far been proposed.

No phase of defense promises a success rate that would allow a layered BMD system to reduce the number of warheads arriving on U.S. territory sufficiently to prevent unprecedented death and destruction. Instead, each phase presents intractable problems, and the resulting failure of the system compounds from one phase to the next. A highly efficient boost-phase intercept is a prerequisite of total BMD but is doomed by the inherent limitations of the weapons, insoluble basing dilemmas, and an array of offensive countermeasures. Because of these, the failure of mid-course systems is preordained. Mid-course BMD is plagued not so much by the laws of physics and geometry as by the sheer unmanageability of the task if a ruthless (but apparently unattainable) thinning out of the attack has not occurred in boost phase. Terminal-phase BMD remains fundamentally unsuitable for area defense of population centers, as opposed to hard-point targets. There seems no way of defending soft targets on a continent-wide basis against the broad variety of attacks that would be tailored to circumvent and overwhelm terminal defenses.

POLITICAL AND STRATEGIC IMPLICATIONS

The political and strategic dangers risked by the "Star Wars" initiative are at least as important as its technical flaws. The most obvious of these political and military hazards are immediate and predictable, in contrast to the putative benefits of BMD, which are distant and hypothetical. Some of the adverse political fallout of a commitment to BMD is already apparent in the responses that it has provoked from Western European leaders. More serious political and military consequences would be felt long before the actual deployment of a BMD.

The most serious consequence of a BMD program is the likely response of the Soviet Union. Moscow cannot be expected to stand idly by while the United States implements a crash program to perfect a viable missile defense. It will almost certainly step up its own efforts to develop a BMD and also initiate a search for offensive countermeasures to any U.S. defense. The probable outcome of such an accelerated arms race will be greater military insecurity for both superpowers.

The Soviet Response to BMD

Thirty years of Cold War have created a cognitive barrier of mistrust that dominates superpower perceptions of each other. Leaders on both sides appear to take for granted the aggressive intentions of the other. Each country seems to view most of its adversary's actions in this light even when such an interpretation is unwarranted by the facts. For this reason, a BMD, which to President Reagan may be an avowedly defensive system, is judged an offensive weapon by the Soviets. In the aftermath of Reagan's "Star Wars" speech, Soviet President Yuri Andropov declared that the Strategic Defense Initiative would only seem defensive to "someone not conversant with these matters."[23] Andropov, Konstantin Chernenko, and other Soviet political and military leaders condemned Reagan's quest for BMD as part of a larger U.S. effort to acquire a first-strike capability: BMD would enable the United States to launch a devastating attack against Soviet strategic forces and defend effectively against a poorly coordinated and limited Soviet retaliatory strike. In the context of the ongoing U.S. nuclear buildup—which goes hand in hand with the conversion of virtually all strategic forces to a counterforce role and the adoption of a "war-fighting" strategic doctrine—such an interpretation is by no means inconsistent with the facts. At the same time, the Soviet Union is no more likely than the United States to accept passively a position of strategic inferiority. In addition to working on its own BMD, the Soviets can be expected to give a high priority to the development and maintenance of forces capable of penetrating or circumventing U.S defenses.[24]

Some White House officials have suggested that a U.S.-Soviet BMD competition would play to U.S. technological strengths. Whether or not this is true, it is clear that the Soviet Union would start a BMD-driven arms race with one very real advantage. Because of the large Soviet lead in missile throw-weight capabilities and the absence of the kinds of political constraints that affect U.S. policymakers, Moscow is in a much better position to carry out a rapid offensive buildup. If the SALT II agreement becomes a dead letter through the development and deployment of a BMD, the Soviet Union would possess an option that the United States does not enjoy: a sudden breakout from the SALT limits on MIRVs. The Soviets could more than double the number of warheads carried by their ICBMs by additional MIRVing of their 308 SS-18 missiles. These are limited under SALT II to ten warheads each but could accommodate up to thirty.

In these circumstances, the Reagan administration's suggestion that BMD might improve the prospects for negotiated force reductions is unrealistic. Even less plausible is the idea that a U.S. BMD could be used as a lever, in the words of the president's science adviser, George Keyworth, to "pressure the Soviets to take our arms reduction proposals more seriously than they do now."[25] The fact is that the administration's own "build-down" proposal would be directly undermined by a U.S. BMD initiative. Build-down emphasizes cuts in the heavy multiple-warhead Soviet ICBMs that threaten U.S. land-based missiles and seeks an overall restructuring of strategic forces away from MIRVed missiles toward smaller, single-warhead ICBMs. But as we have seen, a U.S. commitment to BMD would provide the Soviets with even greater incentives for holding on to their heavy ICBMs and possibly even to increase their number.

If, as is likely, the Soviets augment their offensive strategic capability in response to U.S. development of a BMD, the real outcome of the entire venture would surely be just the reverse of that claimed by the administration. Instead of limiting the damage to the United States that would result from a nuclear war, the ultimate effect of BMD development would be to increase it, possibly by several orders of magnitude. One reason for this is Soviet uncertainty about the effectiveness of U.S. defenses. In order not to take any chances, the Soviets are likely to build up their strategic forces well beyond the level actually required to maintain an effective second-strike capability. If the U.S. defense is anything less than foolproof—which is likely, as we have seen, considering the problems inherent in BMD weapons systems—the number of Soviet warheads detonating over U.S. territory in the course of an attack could be several times what it would be in the absence of a BMD.

The Soviet Union is likely to exaggerate not only the effectiveness of any defense the United States develops but also the progress the United States is making toward perfecting that defense. This is because comparative military assessments are almost always based on "worst case" analysis. As progress toward deployment is unlikely to be symmetrical, the disadvantaged side may well feel driven to do whatever it can to forestall its own expected strategic vulnerability. There would be a certain irony to a superpower confrontation triggered off by a BMD competition, because although ballistic missile defenses might appear effective to an adversary, they are unlikely to be very effective in actuality. The superpower that deploys one first could therefore pay a great political price for its efforts without reaping any real military return.

BMD and Crisis Stability

The dangers associated with BMD would not subside even if the superpowers succeeded in keeping the peace throughout the period in which they were striving to develop and deploy their respective antiballistic missile defenses. If both superpowers had near perfect defenses, the ability of either to penetrate the other's defense with even a few warheads would give it tremendous political-military leverage. Each side would therefore do its best to achieve such a capability and would always live in fear that its adversary was on the verge of achieving a breakthrough in this regard.[26] Such a situation would be far more precarious than today's strategic environment. BMDs in place would also increase the risk of nuclear war at times of U.S.-Soviet confrontation and reduce the chances of controlling hostilities if war did occur.

BMD deployments would intensify mutual pressures to preempt in a crisis. BMD systems would be even more vulnerable than land-based missiles and C[3]I (Command, Control, Communications, and Intelligence). With the exception of a submarine-based pop-up system, technically the most demanding and therefore the least realistic option, all of the proposed BMDs would be designed to operate in space or would require some space-based components. These would include sensors to detect enemy ICBM launches and probably a large number of mirrors to reflect energy beams generated on earth. In low orbits, these components would be vulnerable to attack by missiles launched from high-flying fighter planes.

BMD systems or components in higher, geosynchronous orbits could be destroyed, or the sensors they need to track enemy ICBMs could be degraded, by collision or nuclear explosions set off in space. Either superpower could orbit space mines and detonate them whenever desired by remote control. If both sides had BMDs, either system could easily be used to kill, almost instantly, the other's BMD. Even partially effective BMDs could destroy the adversary's communication, surveillance, and other satellites with great rapidity.

The principal utility of such a defensive system would be as one component of a first-strike strategy, a role indicated both by BMD vulnerability and by the expected poor performance characteristics of BMDs. To be a true defensive weapon, a BMD would have to destroy all or almost all attacking missiles; this is not feasible for a variety of technical reasons. However, a partially effective BMD might have more use against the second strike of an enemy, many or most of whose weapons had already been destroyed. A BMD would therefore not only increase the pressure on political leaders to launch a first strike in a serious crisis but could make such an attack a much more attractive prospect than would otherwise be the case. As this reality would be known to both sides, it would generate even greater pressure to launch a first strike for fear that the adversary was about to do so.

These consequences of BMD run directly counter to the claims of its advocates, who argue that BMD would strengthen deterrence and play an important role in limiting the damage of a nuclear war in the event that deterrence fails. These arguments, it should be noted, are attempts to construct strategic rationales for only modestly capable BMD systems. As such, they represent a massive retreat from President Reagan's vision of transcending the system of nuclear deterrence by making nuclear weapons "impotent and obsolete." These justifications for imperfect BMD systems are nevertheless important to address. As the president's original vision is increasingly understood to be unrealistic, a U.S. BMD program is likely to be promoted primarily on grounds of deterrence and damage-limitation—minimizing the destruction of the United States in the course of a nuclear war. Administration officials and supporters have in fact already begun to argue in these terms during the year since President Reagan's speech.

The assertion that BMD would strengthen nuclear deterrence rests mainly on the claim that it would reduce the vulnerability of U.S. land-based missiles to preemptive attack. By protecting the U.S. ability to retaliate, BMD is supposed to make a Soviet first strike less certain of success and therefore less likely. However, this is an argument for terminal, hard-point defense of U.S. missile silos, not for the layered, area defenses being proposed by the administration. Even terminal defenses can be defeated, although they may complicate an attack and force the adversary to deploy many more warheads to achieve the same level of damage obtainable in the absence of any defenses.[27] But the administration's initiative is vastly more expensive and complex than what would be needed for the protection of retaliatory forces, and it is provocative to the Soviet Union in a way that would reduce, not enhance, deterrence stability.

The damage-limitation justification for BMD is as dubious as the deterrence argument. It has two variants. Proponents of BMD argue that defenses would save U.S. lives in the event of a nuclear war. They also assert that this damage-limitation effect would strengthen deterrence itself by making the threat of nuclear retaliation more credible. BMD partisans who emphasize these points generally subscribe to the theory that credible deterrence requires strategic forces designed for actual war-fighting forces—forces that are capable of being used in a selective and flexible manner. They see BMD as useful not only in limiting population fatalities but also in protecting nuclear command and control systems.

These arguments are implausible in light of the size and destructive power of superpower nuclear arsenals and the compensating adjustments in targeting strategy BMD deployments would almost certainly bring about. Command and control systems are universally conceded to be extremely vulnerable. The same is true of cities. The overkill capacity of both superpowers makes their strategic arsenals so redundant that only a near-perfect defense could hope to reduce urban fatalities appreciably in the event of a major nuclear exchange. One possible Soviet response to a serious U.S. attempt to protect cities would be to target its missiles in such a way as to maximize damage to the U.S. population. The Soviets would need only 5 percent of the ballistic missile warheads they already possess to destroy up to half of the U.S. urban population. Even a 95 percent effective BMD could not therefore save the lives of 120 million Americans, a figure that does not include all the expected subsequent deaths from fire, disease, and social disruption.

The unpalatable but inescapable truth is that the vulnerability of the United States to destruction by Soviet nuclear forces cannot be mitigated by any foreseeable defensive shield as long as nuclear weapons exist in their current numbers. Only if offensive forces were radically reduced, to perhaps a tenth of their present scale, could a moderately effective defense begin to make a dramatic difference in the vulnerability of populations to nuclear destruction. But the prospect of negotiating such a reduction would become virtually nonexistent in the midst of a major U.S.-Soviet BMD competition. It is far more likely that Soviet offensive forces would grow in size in response to BMD deployment.

Contrary to the assumptions of those who view BMD as a useful adjunct to a limited-nuclear-war strategy, it seems likely that BMD deployments would reduce both the incentives and the capabilities of the two superpowers to contain nuclear war below the threshold of all-out exchanges. To the extent that each side sees BMD as a serious threat to its "assured destruction" capability, such defenses invite retargeting in order to retain this destructive capacity. The fewer the number of their warheads that the Soviets could expect to penetrate U.S. defenses, the more tempting it would become to assign these warheads to the softest and most valuable targets—major urban areas. Sheer destruction would thus become an important objective, something currently given low priority in war-fighting strategies.

It is also significant that the space-based command and control systems necessary to limited-war strategies would be put at risk if "Star Wars" defenses were deployed. Plans for controlled, protracted nuclear conflict depend critically on survivable satellites for communications, navigation, early warning, and reconnaissance. However, the growing vulnerability of these systems to attack would be an unavoidable side-effect of the development of space-based BMD. In a strategic environment characterized by space-based missile defenses and unrestricted antisatellite competition, space assets would be particularly inviting targets for attack in the initial stages of a superpower war. This situation would not only exacerbate mutual fears of preemptive attack, a phenomenon we have already described, but would also create incentives to use nuclear forces in massive strikes at the outset of hostilities to take advantage of the capabilities of command and control systems before they are destroyed.

Far from contributing to a strategy of limited nuclear war, BMD points in the opposite direction: toward massive, indiscriminate exchanges and the erosion of control over strategic forces. A nuclear war fought under these circumstances could well produce many more fatalities than one fought in the absence of defenses.

BMD, ASATs, and Arms Control

There is a close link, technologically and strategically, between space-based BMD systems and antisatellite weapons. ASATs are the most obvious countermeasure against space-based BMD systems or components. Technologically, weapons designed for the two missions overlap substantially. U.S. directed-energy programs, including the DARPA (Defense Advanced Research Projects Agency) triad—the Alpha chemical laser, the Large Optics Demonstration Experiment (or LODE), and the Talon Gold system for target acquisition and tracking—have potential applications to both BMD and ASAT systems. Hit-to-kill vehicles, like the Miniature Homing Vehicle (MHV), being developed for U.S. ASAT missions are far less technically demanding than missile defense; the targets are softer, fewer in number, and less time-urgent. Even crude BMD systems might be effective antisatellite weapons. Emerging BMD technologies for terminal and mid-course interception would have considerable capability against satellites in low earth orbits; directed-energy weapons designed to attack missiles in boost phase could threaten early-warning and communications satellites in geosynchronous orbits.[28]

The fact that ASATs and BMDs are based in part on the same technology means that arms control of ASATs, or the lack of it, has major implications for the control of BMD development. Unrestricted ASAT development would undermine the ABM Treaty prohibition of space-based missile defenses; restrictions or a ban on ASATs would reinforce the treaty prohibition and greatly impede progress toward space-based defenses. For this reason, BMD proponents tend to oppose ASAT controls and to regard ASAT development as a technically and legally expedient stepping-stone toward BMD. U.S. officials openly acknowledge that the United States intends to exploit this loophole. George Keyworth has advocated the development of a ground-based laser weapon on these grounds. "It may not necessarily be the best way for the ASAT mission," he admitted, "but a geosynchronous antisatellite capability is important to test the technology to destroy missiles."[29] Development of space-based BMD would forfeit any chance of ASAT control and actually stimulate a competition in ASAT weaponry. This would be detrimental to U.S. interests because the United States relies much more upon satellites than does the Soviet Union to perform the critical national security functions of early warning, military communication, and arms control verification.[30] The U.S. BMD initiative, dangerous in its own right, is also unwise because it precludes the possibility of ASAT control. By the same token, a ban on ASAT is desirable on its own merits and also as a means of closing a dangerous loophole in the ABM Treaty.

The ballistic missile defense envisaged by the Reagan administration poses a particularly grave threat to the future of arms control because it is plainly inconsistent with the 1972 Anti-Ballistic Missile Treaty.[31] The president's own Arms Control Impact Statement for Fiscal Year 1984 recognized that the treaty "bans the development, testing, and deployment of all ABM systems and components that are sea-based, air-based, space-based, or mobile land-based." The Impact Statement also acknowledged that the ban on space systems applies to directed-energy technologies. Under the interpretation of "development" offered by the United States at the time the treaty was signed, the treaty's prohibitions take effect at the point that ABM systems or components enter the phase of field testing.

The ABM Treaty and its 1974 Protocol limit the United States and the Soviet Union to a single ABM deployment area each, which may include up to 100 interceptor missiles.[32] Only the Soviets currently exercise this deployment option: They maintain a terminal defense around Moscow. In the mid-1970s, the United States deactivated its ABM installation at Grand Forks, North Dakota, because it was not judged an effective defense. The treaty permits ABM research and testing subject to a number of serious constraints, including the limit on basing. It also imposes constraints on air-defense systems and early-warning radars in order to limit their possible use in ABM modes. The purpose of all of these restrictions is to enhance the treaty's effectiveness by preventing either superpower from laying the technical groundwork for a "breakout"—renunciation of the pact followed by quick deployment of an extensive ABM system.

The ABM Treaty is important for practical and symbolic reasons. It constitutes mutual recognition and acceptance of three fundamental strategic realities: (1) Effective territorial defense against nuclear weapons is technically infeasible; (2) the pursuit of such a defense would be strategically destabilizing; and (3) such a defense would preclude negotiated constraints on offensive nuclear forces. These premises remain valid, and the ABM Treaty accordingly remains very much in the interest of both superpowers. Renunciation of the treaty by either signatory would be tantamount to a rejection of arms control and would have dangerous political as well as military consequences for U.S.-Soviet relations.

The Reagan BMD initiative, certainly the most serious challenge of the ABM Treaty to date, is neither the first nor only such threat. Ongoing developments in both the United States and the USSR already threaten the treaty's integrity. Of particular concern are the testing of ASATs and of advanced air-defense systems that may have some BMD capability and the recent flurry of charges and counter-charges of treaty violations. Collectively, these developments suggest that a crisis of confidence in the ABM Treaty may be fast approaching. The superpowers must reaffirm their commitment to the treaty or risk its demise—and with it an end to their efforts to regulate strategic weaponry. In the absence of a treaty, each side would feel a growing need to increase its strategic arsenals as a hedge against the prospect of its adversary developing an even partially effective BMD.

The issue of treaty compliance has become particularly troublesome since the United States discovered a large phased-array radar near Abalokova in Siberia, in the vicinity of Soviet ICBM fields. In a January 1984 report alleging Soviet violations of several arms control agreements, the Reagan administration described this radar as "almost certainly" a violation of the ABM Treaty.[33] The possibility of Soviet violations of the ABM Treaty is a matter of serious concern and ought to be pursued diligently by the United States. However, it is important to bear in mind that none of the Soviet activities in question pose a militarily significant threat. Nor does existing evidence at all support the view that the Soviets are preparing for a breakout from the treaty. On the contrary, there is good reason to believe that Moscow continues to value the treaty, not the least as a means of containing superior U.S. technology. From this standpoint, the Soviets are probably anxious to forestall the kind of BMD competition that a breakdown of the ABM Treaty would stimulate. The spate of recent Soviet initiatives aimed at a moratorium on ASAT testing and a comprehensive ban on space weapons certainly supports this inter-pretation.

One thing seems certain: There can be no hope of resolving questions about Soviet compliance with the ABM Treaty so long as the United States maintains a presidential-level commitment to a major BMD effort. The administration cannot have it both ways. It cannot pursue a goal that is openly in conflict with the treaty while invoking the treaty against the Soviet Union. Secretary of Defense

Caspar Weinberger has attempted to reconcile this contradiction with the assertion that a BMD program "can be fully pursued for the next several years within existing treaty constraints."[34] His claim is disingenuous on two counts. In the first place, it is not apparent that even the near-term activities planned by the United States can be reconciled with the ABM Treaty. At the very least, demonstrations of certain key technologies, such as the Talon Gold tracking system or a ground-based ASAT laser, are legally questionable. In the opinion of many experts, such demonstrations would violate the treaty because they would constitute field testing of BMD components. Of perhaps even greater significance, a political commitment to pursue BMD could make the issue of near-term compliance almost irrelevant by signaling to the Soviet Union that ultimate U.S. abrogation of the treaty is highly likely. In these circumstances, the treaty could lose its authority well before the United States crossed the line of clearly proscribed activities.

Superpower BMD deployments would also have an adverse impact on the prospects for theater nuclear-arms control. Great Britain and France, and China as well, would feel threatened by Soviet development of a missile defense that undercut the ability of their ICBMs to destroy Soviet targets. All three countries could be expected to modernize and possibly to expand their nuclear arsenals in order to maintain the minimum deterrence their nuclear strategies seek to achieve. France, for example, has insisted that as a precondition for participation in future euromissile negotiations "defensive systems . . . must remain limited."[35]

BMD and the Alliance

The North Atlantic Treaty Organization (NATO) has suffered a series of political tremors in the course of the last decade, all of which have been damaging to the foundations of alliance solidarity. Some of the worst of these tremors have had their epicenter in Washington, among them the neutron bomb debacle, the failure of SALT II to gain ratification, and the loose language of the Reagan administration about the feasibility of a limited nuclear war in Europe.

Many West Europeans, perhaps a majority of those who express an opinion on the subject, believe that the United States bears the onus for the failure of the SALT process. The Reagan administration is singled out for criticism in this regard because so many of its most prominent foreign policy and defense officials fought against SALT II prior to the 1980 election. Some of them were subsequently put in charge of arms control negotiations. Not surprisingly, the administration has not succeeded in convincing too many Europeans of the sincerity of its commitment to the arms control process. It remains to be seen whether or not the current round of arms talks will in any way allay this suspicion.

Reagan's anti-arms control image has had a profound political effect in Europe. In tandem with the series of statements by White House officials in 1980–1982 that suggested that the United States was complacent about nuclear risks, it has been a major catalyst for the growth of powerful peace movements everywhere in Northern Europe. These movements have attempted to halt the deployment of a new generation of U.S. nuclear weapons (intermediate-range nuclear force—INF) in Europe: the 108 Pershing IIs to be stationed in the Federal Republic of Germany and 454 cruise missiles that will also go into West Germany, the Netherlands, Great Britain, and Italy. The success of the peace movements in mobilizing widespread opposition to INF modernization was greatly if unintentionally facilitated by the public justification that the NATO Council of Foreign Ministers offered for its December 1979 decision to deploy these weapons. They were to be part of a "two-track" strategy of arms control negotiations and nuclear-force modernization. By demonstrating alliance resolve, the agreement to deploy these weapons was expected to make the Soviets take theater arms control negotiations seriously. NATO officials and some European political leaders even maintained that actual deployment of the Pershings and cruise missiles would probably not be necessary because the very fact of a West European commitment to deploy them would probably be sufficient to secure the kind of arms control agreement that would make INF modernization unnecessary. The new weapons were therefore sold as a bargaining chip. As the Reagan administration appears to many Europeans to have violated its part of the bargain by sabotaging the arms control process, the Europeans feel quite justified in opposing the deployment of new nuclear weapons.

The peace movements and related opposition to INF modernization have not prevented the actual deployment of these weapons. The first Pershing IIs are now in place in West Germany, and cruise missiles are currently being deployed in Great Britain and West Germany. However, the controversy surrounding deployment has shattered whatever previous consensus on defense issues existed in these countries. For European conservatives, the Soviet threat remains prominent and requires concerted military and political action in order to strengthen NATO's capability and resolve in the eyes of Moscow. For many on the Left, the superpowers are seen to constitute equal threats to the peace of Europe, a sentiment that finds political expression in a desire to weaken the military, political, and economic ties of their respective countries with the United States. This division is especially pronounced in the Federal Republic of Germany and Great Britain, to the general detriment of those political leaders who favor a strong defense and alliance. In West Germany, the division helped bring about the fall of Chancellor Helmut Schmidt, who was subsequently unable to prevent his own Social Democratic party, now in opposition, from voting against INF. In Great Britain, the Labour party, also in opposition, has moved further to the Left and is now officially committed to unilateral nuclear disarmament.

In the opinion of most observers, NATO is in as great a state of political disarray as it has been at any time during its thirty-six-year history. Its survival is not at stake—no one expects the alliance to collapse in the near future—but rather its effectiveness as a political and military organization. A U.S. commitment to BMD, followed by abrogation—de facto or de jure—of the existing ABM Treaty, would magnify enormously the already existing divisions among Europeans and might just make NATO's survival a real political question. At the very least, such events would further erode political support for the alliance in Western Europe. Europeans have a continuing concern for arms control, especially of theater-based systems, which is seen not only as a mechanism for limiting the destructiveness of any war fought in Europe but, more important, as a means of preventing such a war to the extent that it helps to reduce East-West tensions. A U.S. commitment to BMD would be interpreted as extremely damaging to both objectives; it would be seen to signal an end to arms control and the beginning of a new and dangerous arms race.

European leaders have already begun to express their concern. In the Federal Republic of Germany, the country most sensitive to the state of East-West relations, U.S. talk of ballistic missile defense at first produced a rare consensus among political leaders. In April 1984, West German Defense Minister Manfred Wörner, upon his return from a meeting of NATO's nuclear planning group, announced to the press that U.S. efforts to develop BMD could "destabilize the East-West balance" and dramatically increase tensions with Moscow. Karsten Voigt, foreign policy spokesman for the opposition Social Democrats, predicted that if Washington proceeds with its plan to develop space weapons it would set off a storm of public protests and trigger a serious confrontation between West Germany and the United States. At the other end of the political spectrum, Franz Josef Strauss, head of the conservative Christian Socialist Union, declared that the Reagan administration's space programs represent a unilateral rejection of the U.S.-European partnership, something that could threaten the survival of the alliance.[36]

Many West Europeans also fear that BMD signifies a retreat into a "fortress America" mentality, and with it a sacrifice of important European interests for the sake of greater U.S. security. In the opinion of Dutch Defense Minister Jacob de Ruiter, it makes Europeans uneasy that a missile defense system protecting the United States would leave Europe vulnerable.[37] Other Europeans have taken this argument a step further and worry aloud that a partially protected United States might be more willing to risk war with the Soviet Union, a war that would almost surely result in Europe's destruction.

Secretary of Defense Caspar Weinberger has attempted to assure NATO leaders that a U.S. BMD would protect Europe as well as the United States.[38] However, this appears to be another of the administration's facile promises. The technical obstacles to defending Europe are significantly greater than those standing in the way of defending the continental United States. Most of the nuclear weapons that the Soviet Union would use against Western Europe would be delivered by aircraft or theater-based missile systems. Aircraft are not subject to interdiction by BMDs and have shown an enduring ability to penetrate the most sophisticated antiaircraft defenses that either superpower has devised. Once again, anything short of a 100 percent effective system, a practical impossibility in any case, would not save European cities and major military assets from destruction.

In the case of missiles, the problem is compounded by the relatively short distances between launchers and targets in the European theater, anywhere between 50 and 2,000 kilometers. The shorter distance permits a shorter boost stage, a lower trajectory, and less overall time elapsed between launch and impact. The SS-20, for example, has a flight time of between five and ten minutes to West European targets. The SS-22s, reportedly being deployed in Eastern Europe, could reach their targets in about three minutes. Boost-stage defenses would be useless against such weapons.[39] The Soviets could also field systems that made use of depressed trajectories, something that would further complicate interception, if not make interception by BMDs altogether impossible.

According to press reports, European leaders remain unimpressed by · Weinberger's assertions of the need for BMD. Prime Minister Margaret Thatcher of Great Britain and Defense Minister Wörner of the Federal Republic of Germany have nevertheless, at Washington's prodding, come out in support of the research effort to develop BMD. At the same time, however, they reaffirmed their respective commitments to arms control agreements that would ban the deployment of such weapons.[40] The British and West German governments continue to doubt Weinberger's claim that Europe would come under a U.S. BMD umbrella.[41] It is clear that the Reagan administration will trigger a serious crisis of confidence on the other side of the Atlantic if it pushes ahead with BMD at the expense of arms control.

CONCLUSION

The overall consequences of a commitment to BMD would be just the opposite of those predicted by its proponents. Instead of making the United States more secure it would set in motion a chain of events that would leave both superpowers considerably less secure. Deterrence would be weakened and crisis instability increased, making the prospect of a war more likely. Damage limitation would be undermined by the need of both sides to increase their strategic arsenals in order to compensate for each other's defenses. Both sides could also be expected to target more of their missiles against cities, which would still remain the most vulnerable of targets. BMD requires abrogation of the ABM Treaty and would thus sound the death knell to the arms control process. This would trigger a new round of the arms race and extend military competition into space. Defensive systems would also require vast expenditures for research, development, testing, deployment, and maintenance, with very little to show for this expenditure. Finally, a commitment to BMD would provoke a serious crisis in the Atlantic alliance; regardless of its ultimate outcome, such a crisis would leave NATO and the United States in a weakened position militarily and politically. The late Republican senator Arthur Vandenberg was fond of attacking schemes he opposed by declaring "the end unattainable, the means hairbrained, and the cost staggering." For Vandenberg, this was a politically useful form of exaggeration. For BMD, it is an entirely fitting description.

NOTES

1. *New York Times*, 24 March 1983, p. 1; Weinberger appeared on "Meet the Press" on 27 March 1983. The following analysis draws heavily on the Union of Concerned Scientists, *The Fallacy of Star Wars* (New York: Vintage Books, 1984), to which the author contributed.

2. See, for example, Kurt Gottfried, Henry W. Kendall, Hans A. Bethe, Richard L. Garwin, Noel Gayler, Richard Ned Lebow, Carl Sagan, and Victor Weisskopf, *Space-Based Missile Defense* (Cambridge: Union of Concerned Scientists, March 1984). A revised and expanded version of this report was published in October 1984 under the title, *The Fallacy of Star Wars.* See also Ashton B. Carter, *Directed Energy Missile Defense in Space: Missile Defense in Space,* Background Paper prepared for the Office of Technology Assessment of the Congress of the United States (Washington, D.C.: Government Printing Office, 1984); Sidney Drell, Philip J. Farley, and David Holloway, *The Reagan Strategic Defense Initiative: A Technical, Political, and Arms Control*

Assessment (Stanford, Calif.: Center for International Security and Arms Control, 1984); and Jeffrey Boutwell and Donald Hafner, eds., *Space Weapons: A Study Prepared for the American Academy of Arts and Sciences* (New York: W. W. Norton, 1985). A group of Soviet scientists, led by Academician R. Z. Sagdeev, director of the Institute of Space Research of the Soviet Academy of Sciences, and Dr. A. A. Kokoshin of the Institute of the United States and Canada, has also issued a report disparaging the technical feasibility of a BMD, "Prospects for the Creation of a U.S. Space Based Ballistic Missile Defence System and the Likely Impact of Soviet Scientists in Defence of Peace and Against the Threat of Nuclear War," mimeographed (Moscow: 1983). E. P. Velikov, vice-president of the Soviet Academy of Sciences, has also dismissed an effective BMD as "just a pipe dream"; see his article in the *Washington Post,* 24 June 1984, p. B5. For favorable analyses, see U.S., House of Representatives, Committee on Armed Services, Subcommittee on Research and Development, 98th Congress, 2d sess., statements by James C. Fletcher, Richard D. DeLauer, and Gerold Yonas (Washington, D.C.: Government Printing Office, 1 March 1984); John C. Toomay, "The Case For A Ballistic-Missile-Defense-Oriented World," and Gerold Yonas, "The Strategic Defense Initiative," in Boutwell and Hafner, *Space Weapons.*

3. For a concise description of the SDI research effort see the statement referred to above by Richard D. DeLauer, under secretary of defense for research and engineering, before the Committee on Armed Services. For a more technical description of some of the individual research projects, see Clarence A. Robinson, Jr., "BMD Research Draws Strategic Focus," *Aviation Week and Space Technology,* 18 June 1984, pp. 83–93.

4. *Aviation Week and Space Technology,* 18 June 1984, pp. 19–20. The army's Homing Overlay Experiment (HOE) on 10 June 1984 destroyed a dummy Minuteman RV at least 160 kilometers (100 miles) above the Pacific launched some twenty minutes earlier from California. The homing interceptor was launched with a Minuteman booster from Kwajalein; before impact a 5-meter (16.3-foot) diameter metallic framework is deployed to greatly increase the kill area. As a satellite is much larger and more fragile than an RV, there is no doubt that this weapon has an ASAT capability. (This system is described in Union of Concerned Scientists, *The Fallacy of Star Wars,* pp. 179–185.)

5. Union of Concerned Scientists, *The Fallacy of Star Wars,* pp. 214–227. See Ashton B. Carter, "The Relationship of ASAT and BMD," in Boutwell and Hafner, *Space Weapons,* for a discussion of both the technical relationship between ASAT and BMD and the implications of this for arms control.

6. On the Johnson administration and ABM, see Benson D. Adams, "McNamara's ABM Policy, 1961–1967," *Orbis* 12 (Spring 1968), pp. 200–225; Ralph E. Lapp, "A Biography of ABM," *New York Times Magazine,* 4 May 1969; Morton H. Halperin, "The Decision to Deploy the ABM: Bureaucratic and Domestic Politics in the Johnson Administration," *World Politics* 25 (October 1972), pp. 62–95; Phil Williams and Stephen Kirby, "The ABM and American Domestic Politics," *Arms Control* 3 (September 1982), pp. 50–72; David N. Schwartz, "Past and Present: The Historical Legacy," in Ashton B. Carter and David N. Schwartz, eds., *Ballistic Missile Defense* (Washington, D.C.: Brookings Institution, 1984), pp. 330–349.

7. See Sayre Stevens, "The Soviet BMD Program," in Carter and Schwartz, *Ballistic Missile Defense,* pp. 182–220; Drell, Farley, and Holloway, *The Reagan Strategic Defense Initiatives,* pp. 13–29.

8. Solly Zuckerman, *Nuclear Illusion and Reality* (New York: Vintage Books, 1982), p. 51.

9. Thomas B. Cochran, William M. Arkin, and Milton M. Hoenig, *Nuclear Weapons Databook,* Vol. I: *U.S. Nuclear Forces and Capabilities* (Cambridge: Ballinger, 1984), pp. 121, 127.

10. This is the figure used in the Fletcher Report. This official investigation of BMD by the Defensive Technologies Study Team was headed by James C. Fletcher and has provided technical guidance on the Strategic Defense Initiative to the Defense and Energy Departments. For a summary, see Dr. Fletcher's statement on the Strategic Defense Initiative before the House Committee on Armed Services, cited above.

11. On terminal defenses, see Stephen Weiner, "Systems and Technology," and Ashton B. Carter, "BMD Applications: Performance and Limitations," in Carter and Schwartz, *Ballistic Missile Defense,* pp. 49–97, 98–181.

12. Union of Concerned Scientists, *The Fallacy of Star Wars,* p. 142.

13. Ibid., pp. 99–104; Hans A. Bethe, Richard L. Garwin, Kurt Gottfried, and Henry W. Kendall, "Space-Based Ballistic-Missile Defense," *Scientific American* 251 (October 1984), pp. 39–49.

14. Union of Concerned Scientists, *The Fallacy of Star Wars,* pp. 104–110.

15. For technical details and further discussion of lasers and particle beams, see M. Callaham and Kosta Tsipis, "High Energy Laser Weapons: A Technical Assessment," Report No. 6, Program in Science and Technology for International Security (Cambridge: Massachusetts Institute of Technology, Dept. of Physics, 1980); Union of Concerned Scientists, *The Fallacy of Star Wars,* pp. 66–143; Drell, Farley, and Holloway, *The Reagan Strategic Defense Initiative,* pp. 39–63; Hans A. Bethe and Richard L. Garwin, "New BMD Technologies," in Boutwell and Hafner, *Space Weapons.*

16. This relationship is expressed by the formula

$$d = 1.3 \, (w/D)R$$

where w is the wavelength of the light, d and D are the diameters of the spot and mirror respectively, and R is the range, or distance from the mirror to the target.

17. George Keyworth, *Reassessing Strategic Defense* (Washington, D.C.: Council on Foreign Relations, 1984), p. 12; Drell, Farley, and Holloway, *The Reagan Strategic Defense Initiative,* pp. 56–57.

18. Clarence A. Robinson, Jr., "Defense Dept. Developing Orbital Guns," *Aviation Week and Space Technology,* 23 July 1984, pp. 61–69.

19. Robert Cooper, director of the Defense Advanced Research Projects Agency (DARPA), testified before the Senate Armed Services Committee on 2 May 1983 that no fewer than 25,000 railguns would have to be put into space! U.S., Senate, Committee on Armed Services, 98th Congress, 1st sess., *Strategic and Theater Nuclear Forces,* Hearings on Department of Defense Authorization for Appropriations for Fiscal Year 1984, March-May 1983 (Washington, D.C.: Government Printing Office, 1983), p. 2891.

20. Richard Halloran, "Higher Budget Foreseen for Advanced Missiles," *New York Times,* 18 May 1983, p. 11.

21. "Short Burn Time ICBM Considerations," presented to the Defensive Technology Study Team (Fletcher Commission), 20 July 1983, by Martin Marietta, Denver Aerospace.

22. See Louis Goldman, "Is There a Soviet Bomb in Wichita?," *Bulletin of the Atomic Scientists* 40 (January 1984), pp. 54–55.

23. *Pravda,* 27 March 1983. Reprinted as "Andropov Interviewed on U.S. Military Policy," *FBIS,* 28 March 1983, USSR International Affairs, pp. A1–A3. For a fuller treatment of the Soviet reaction, see Drell, Farley, and Holloway, *The Reagan Strategic Defense Initiative,* pp. 22–29.

24. *New York Times,* 1 February 1985, p. A3.

25. *National Journal,* 7 January 1984, p. 14.

26. This point is made nicely by Charles L. Glaser, "Why Even Good Defenses May Be Bad," *International Security* 9 (Fall 1984), pp. 92–123.

27. On this point see Carter, "BMD Applications: Performance and Limitations," in Carter and Schwartz, *Ballistic Missile Defense,* pp. 98–181.

28. See n. 5, above.

29. Quoted in *Aviation Week and Space Technology,* 18 July 1983, p. 21.

30. See Kurt Gottfried and Richard Ned Lebow, "Anti-Satellite Weapons: Military Opportunity or Political-Military Blunder?" in Boutwell and Hafner, *Space Weapons,* for an analysis of the relative dependence, today and a decade from now, of the superpowers on satellites.

31. For documentation, see U.S., Senate, 98th Congress, 1st sess., "Outer Space Arms Control Negotiations," Report of the Committee on Foreign Relations (Washington, D.C.: Government Printing Office, 1983); Alan B. Sherr, "Legal Issues of the 'Star Wars' Defense Program" (Boston: Lawyers Alliance for Nuclear Arms Control, June 1984); Union of Concerned Scientists, *The Fallacy of Star Wars,* pp. 167–172; Drell, Farley, and Holloway, *The Reagan Strategic Initiative,* pp. 7–38, 81–92.

32. This treaty and its protocol are to be found in U.S., Arms Control and Disarmament Agency, *Arms Control and Disarmament Agreements: Texts and Histories of Negotiations* (Washington, D.C.: Government Printing Office, 1980), pp. 132–147, 161–163.

33. U.S., Senate, 98th Congress, 1st sess., "Soviet Treaty Violations," Testimony before the Armed Services Committee (Washington, D.C.: Government Printing Office, March 1984); Michael Krepon, "Decontrolling the Arms Race: The U.S. and Soviets Fumble the Compliance Issue," *Arms Control Today* 14 (March-April 1984), pp. 1–9; Thomas Longstreth, John Pike, and John Rhinelander, "A Report on the Impact of U.S. and Soviet Missile Defense Programs on the ABM Treaty" (Washington, D.C.: The National Campaign to Save the ABM Treaty, March 1985).

34. *Report of the Secretary of Defense Caspar W. Weinberger to the Congress on the FY 1985 Budget, FY 1986 Authorization Request and FY 1985–89 Defense Programs,* 1 February 1984, p. 193.

35. *New York Times,* 2 October 1983.

36. *Der Spiegel,* 4 April 1984, p. 120, 12 November 1984, pp. 136–147; *New York Times,* 10 April 1984, p. 6; *Washington Post,* 11 April 1984, p. A30; *Christian Science Monitor,* 12 April 1984, p. 1; *Boston Globe,* 30 July 1984, p. 2.

37. *Washington Post,* 4 April 1984, p. 18.

38. *Washington Post,* 11 April 1984, p. 29; George Keyworth has repeated this assertion (*Baltimore Sun,* 9 July 1984, p. 1).

39. *New York Times,* 23 July 1984, p. 19.

40. *Wall Street Journal,* 4 April 1984, p. 33; *Christian Science Monitor,* 12 April 1984, p. 1.

41. *Der Spiegel,* 12 November 1984, pp. 136–147; *Baltimore Sun,* 13 July 1984, p. 2.

6

STRATEGIC ARMS LIMITATION NEGOTIATIONS AND U.S. DECISION MAKING

ROBERT A. HOOVER

In December 1984 President Ronald Reagan announced that the Soviet Union and the United States would return to the bargaining tables to resume the Strategic Arms Reduction Talks (START). The announcement, in conjunction with general public concern about the poor record of strategic arms limitation during the preceding decade, has sparked renewed interest in analyzing the possibilities for effective strategic arms control. In contrast to early arms control analysis, which focused exclusively on strategic theory[1] and later highlighted the complexities of the technology,[2] it has become increasingly evident to analysts that the domestic politics of national security decision making constitutes a significant and complex dimension of the arms control process.[3] Consequently, for the United States to pursue strategic arms limitation with the Soviet Union in an effective way requires an understanding of how the U.S. decision-making process for arms limitation operates.

National security policy analysts tend to utilize one of two paradigms to explain U.S. national security policy decision making: the presidential paradigm[4] or the bureaucratic politics paradigm.[5] One assumption common to both is that national security policy is conceived and processed in ways strikingly different from domestic policy. Both paradigms emphasize personal factors and factors relating to the executive branch in explaining decision making. They consider institutions other than the executive branch and other factors associated with domestic politics as unimportant. Although the presidential and bureaucratic politics paradigms are fundamentally different, proponents of both argue that policy conceived and processed under the assumptions of the preferred paradigm significantly enhances the effectiveness of U.S. national security policy.

However, neither paradigm adequately explains U.S. national security decision making as it relates to strategic arms limitation since 1966. Although each paradigm offers insight into U.S. strategic arms limitation decision making at certain times, at critical junctures the decision making more closely resembles domestic decision making. When this is so, coalition politics transcends institutional boundaries, socioeconomic considerations and political interests become germane, the electoral and lobbying processes become influential, and the concerns for broader societal impacts of policy choices become critical.[6]

This chapter explores the following questions about these two explanations of U.S. strategic arms limitation decision making: (1) What are the general propositions of the two paradigms? (2) Are the paradigms deficient in explaining U.S. strategic arms limitation decision making? (3) If so, what factors limit the paradigms in explaining U.S. strategic arms limitation decision making? (4) What are the implications of this analysis for future U.S. strategic arms limitation decision making?

DECISION-MAKING PARADIGMS

Several analysts have suggested that the bureaucratic politics paradigm is the most frequently used decision-making framework in social science.[7] It is used to describe, explain, and predict the actions of the United States in Cold War crises, foreign policy decisions, and procurement activities. It largely dominated the national security decision-making literature following the studies of Samuel Huntington, Paul Hammond, and others that appeared in the late 1950s and early 1960s. A decade later, Graham Allison and Morton Halperin refined and formalized these scholars' arguments.[8] Seven propositions compose the core of the bureaucratic politics paradigm.

1. Policymaking is confined to a small group of individuals and organizations within the executive branch arena.

2. In the consideration of any single issue, the executive branch is composed of individuals and organizations with differing goals and objectives. These individuals and organizations respond to any single issue in ways that reflect their desire and

need to advance either their individual interests or those of the mission of their organizations, or both. Conflict arises over these differing views about national security policy issues, i.e., stakes. "Where you stand on an issue depends on where you sit." Nevertheless, these conflicts are intra–executive branch rather than intragovernmental.

3. National security policy decisions are the result of bargaining and compromise that occur within the executive branch arena over these differing interests.

4. Although all individuals and organizations are not equal in the bargaining and compromise that marks conflict over policy, the president is not the dominant individual in the policy struggle that results from differing goals and objectives within the executive branch.

5. The relative influence of individuals and organizations over the policy struggle depends upon (a) the interest and power of the agency responsible for the procurement decision under consideration; (b) the skills of the actors and organizations, particularly the mobilizing allies among key executive branch officials and outside the executive arena; and (c) the existence of external forces or threats reaffirming the needs of a certain agency, e.g., evidence of advances in Soviet technology compelling enough to warrant innovative changes in U.S. weapons technology. From this perspective, the president is viewed as "wearing sneakers rather than riding boots."

6. Controversy exists as to whether the bargaining and compromising over national security policy decision making has positive or negative normative implications. On the one hand, competition within the executive branch over national security policy may produce a healthy review of the advantages and disadvantages of various alternatives. On the other hand, national security decision making characterized by bargaining and compromise may inhibit coherence, consistency, continuity, and purposive action in U.S. national security policy—values highly prized by many foreign policy analysts.

7. Domestic factors and forces are essentially ancillary to the decision-making process for national security policy decision making. More precisely, Congress and the general public are deferential and supportive of executive prerogative in this policy area; most interest groups lack the interest, experience, and/or

knowledge to actively lobby; and if members of Congress become involved, they do so for reason of pork barrel as opposed to strategic considerations.[9]

The presidential politics paradigm for U.S. national security decision making is used by two groups of analysts. First, those individuals seeking to refocus the debate on the necessity of coherence, continuity, consistency, and purposive action argue that the bureaucratic politics paradigm constitutes a dangerous excuse for avoiding responsibility.[10] Second, other analysts indicate that the presidential politics paradigm is a better descriptive framework than the bureaucratic politics paradigm.[11] Seven propositions form the core of the presidential politics paradigm.

1. Policymaking is confined to a small group of individuals and organizations within the executive branch arena.

2. In the consideration of any single issue, the executive branch is composed of individuals and organizations with similar goals and objectives. Where an "individual or organization stands on an issue depends on where the president appointed the individual or organization to sit." Conflict may arise over differing views about national security policy issues. Furthermore, these conflicts are intra–executive branch rather than intragovernmental.

3. The president is the dominant individual in the policy struggle within the executive branch. If the president chooses to be interested in a policy issue, he has the resources and power to effect policy decisively.

4. National security policy decisions reflect the interests of the president when the president so chooses. Otherwise, national security policy decisions are the result of bargaining and compromise that occur within the executive branch arena over differing interests.

5. When bargaining and compromise occur, the relative influence of individuals and organizations over the policy struggle depends upon (a) the interest and power of the agency responsible for the procurement decision under consideration; (b) the skills of the actors and organizations, particularly in mobilizing allies among key executive branch officials and outside the executive arena; and (c) the existence of external forces or threats reaffirming the needs of a certain agency, e.g., evidence of advances

in Soviet technology compelling enough to warrant innovative changes in U.S. weapons technology. From this perspective, the president is viewed as "wearing sneakers rather than riding boots."

6. Controversy exists as to whether presidential dominance over national security policy decision making has positive or negative normative implications. On the one hand, presidential dominance encourages coherence, consistency, continuity, and purposive action in U.S. national security policy—values highly prized by these foreign policy analysts. On the other hand, hierarchy within the executive branch produces policy without a healthy review of alternatives and may result in tunnel vision.

7. Domestic factors and forces are essentially ancillary to the decision-making process for national security policy decision making. More precisely, Congress and the general public are deferential and supportive of executive prerogative in the policy area; most interest groups lack the interest, experience, and/or knowledge to actively lobby; and if members of Congress become involved, they do so for reason of pork barrel as opposed to strategic considerations.[12]

The next task is to determine whether either paradigm adequately explains the pattern of strategic arms control decision making since the 1960s.

SALT AND START EPISODES

I have divided this review of U.S. strategic arms limitation decision making into six episodes, each resembling, in varying degrees, either one of the paradigms or a pattern of domestic decision making. These episodes consider: the first Nixon administration and SALT I; the Johnson administration, ABM, and SALT planning; the 1966–1967 ABM (antiballistic missile) and strategic arms limitation decisions; the Nixon and Ford administrations and SALT II (balanced asymmetries and equal aggregates); the Carter administration and SALT II (the September compromise); and the Reagan administration and the MX/START compromise.

The First Nixon Administration:
The Verification Panel and SALT I

U.S. strategic arms limitation policy decision making during the first Nixon administration more closely resembled the propositions of the presidential politics paradigm than did perhaps any other episode in U.S. arms control history.[13] The president and his national security adviser, Henry Kissinger, were vitally interested in and committed to integrating U.S. arms control policy with their policy of détente toward the Soviet Union. The strategy for implementing détente required that SALT policy be planned and tightly controlled by the president and his national security adviser.

During the first months of 1969, as the administration prepared for the coming SALT negotiations with the Soviets, Nixon and Kissinger were annoyed by the bureaucratic conflict between the Pentagon and the State Department/Arms Control and Disarmament Agency (ACDA). They felt conflict would produce a diluted U.S. negotiating position marred by bureaucratic compromise. To counter this, Nixon and Kissinger brought SALT planning under the control of the newly established Verification Panel chaired by Kissinger. Moreover, later in the administration Nixon and Kissinger initiated direct negotiations with Soviet Ambassador Anatoly Dobrynin, Foreign Minister Andrei Gromyko, and Premier Leonid Brezhnev by the so-called back-channel. Nixon's and Kissinger's control over the planning and execution was so extensive that few beyond their immediate advisers knew the details or character of most U.S. initiatives in the SALT negotiations, at least in the beginning.

This penchant for secrecy and control meant that officials outside the executive branch were not involved in the SALT negotiations. For example, members of the responsible committees in Congress had virtually no interaction with Kissinger during this period. Without periodic consultation with the national security adviser—the key presidential adviser on SALT—Congress lacked direct information about the SALT negotiations. Pentagon officials also often lacked access to the details of the SALT negotiations, especially the back-channel talks. To combat this, a Pentagon person on Kissinger's staff allegedly copied secret documents about SALT and then circulated them in the Pentagon.[14] Moreover, the director of ACDA and ambassador to SALT, Gerard Smith, revealed that even the negotiating team was occasionally in the dark about new U.S. negotiating initiatives.[15] In fact, at least until late 1971 and early 1972, little information existed outside the inner circle of the administration as to the objectives and specifics of the SALT negotiations.

Thus, during this period the strategic arms limitation negotiations received little attention either in Congress or in the national print media. Although questions were raised within the administration about the thrust of the Nixon/Kissinger SALT policy, the absence of specific information about the negotiations restricted the debate.

Moreover, the foreign policy implications of SALT were lost in the wake of the excitement generated by the establishment of talks with the People's Republic of China and the general ambiance surrounding the détente initiatives with the Soviet Union. In addition, the subject of Vietnam dominated the time and interests of the foreign policy community as had no other event since World War II.[16] Finally, during the first years of the Nixon administration, what concern existed about the arms race focused on the ABM. SALT simply was not visible enough to excite public interest. Until the treaty and executive agreement of SALT I came before the Congress in the fall of 1972, Congress was little involved in SALT decision making. Throughout this period, strategic arms limitation decision making reflected the general pattern suggested by the presidential politics paradigm. Coherence and purposive action directed by the president were more nearly achieved in those years than during perhaps any other period.

The Johnson Administration, ABM, and SALT Planning

SALT decision making during the 1967–1968 period of the Johnson administration was a major case study for one of the principal analysts of the bureaucratic politics paradigm.[17] Morton Halperin suggested that following the December 1966 meeting between President Johnson, Secretary of Defense Robert S. McNamara, and the Joint Chiefs of Staff (JCS) in Texas, the administration continued research and development on ABM while simultaneously initiating discussions with the Soviet Union about mutual limitations on the deployment of ABM. After the Glassboro Conference of June 1967 between President Johnson and Soviet Premier Aleksey Kosygin, the United States prepared for extended negotiations with the Soviets. Washington and Moscow eventually agreed that formal discussions would begin in August 1968. The preparation of the U.S. negotiating position for those talks was pursued in classic bureaucratic politics fashion. However, the initiation of the formal talks was postponed following the Soviet invasion of Czechoslovakia in August 1968.

The preparation of the U.S. negotiating position was undertaken by an intergovernmental committee. Johnson sought to obtain from the OSD (Office of the Secretary of Defense), the JCS, the Department of State, ACDA, and the CIA (Central Intelligence Agency) a unified position that could be negotiated with the Soviets. Because he apparently had no clear vision about the character of the agreement and lacked the energy to push a position through the bureaucracy, the president asked the key elements of the bureaucracy with an institutional interest in strategic weapons to provide a unified view for negotiations with the Soviets. These individuals and organizations, of course, had definite and differing views about arms control. Consequently, bureaucratic conflict was inevitable. In the bargaining and compromise process within the intergovernmental committee, chaired by Morton Halperin from the OSD (not the president's staff), the JCS clearly had a power base that enlarged its influence on the committee.

The strategic arms limitation issue during 1967–1968 did not excite much interest in either Congress or the public media. The issue of Vietnam dwarfed all other national security issues during that period. In addition, the JCS's role in the intergovernmental arms limitation committee implied that ABM would not be negotiated away with the Soviets. Moreover, Johnson had bowed to pressure from the JCS, senior senators, and political advisers concerned about the upcoming presidential election and opted to build a limited ABM system. Secretary of Defense McNamara announced the decision in September 1967. The key southern senators, instrumental in the 1966 decision to accelerate the ABM research and development program while simultaneously exploring strategic arms limitation with the Soviets, were pacified and generally uninvolved in the preparation of a SALT position.

Thus, the combination of the president's approach to arms control and the general public's indifference to the arms control issue left the formulation of a negotiating position to classic bureaucratic politics. Furthermore, in neither the Nixon case nor that of the aborted Johnson effort in 1967–1968 was consultation with Congress about an arms control treaty—an agreement that would require either two-thirds approval by the Senate (treaty) or majority approval by both Houses (an executive agreement)—a factor in the thinking of either administration.

The 1966–1967 ABM and Strategic
Arms Limitation Decisions

It is often overlooked that the decision by the Johnson administration to pursue continued research and development of ABM while exploring with the Soviet Union an agreement to limit ABM was not a typical bureaucratic politics activity.[18] As Halperin observes, Lyndon Johnson played a very significant role in the ABM decision making of 1966–1967.[19] He was confronted on the one hand by a united JCS who emphatically supported the deployment of an area ABM system, a weapon system that would provide the U.S. army with the capability to defend the U.S. population against a Soviet nuclear attack. The air force supported the area defense ABM system as an alternative to an ABM defense of Minuteman intercontinental ballistic missiles (ICBMs). The Minuteman would rival future improved ICBMs for funds within the Pentagon. The navy wanted to maintain a united JCS and thus threw support to the army's ABM plan. The funds for the army's ABM would come from the Pentagon's strategic allocation. Thus, regular army officers did not see ABM as a threat to their more traditional programs.

In the Senate, senior senators such as the chairman of the Armed Services Committee Richard Russell, John Stennis, Henry Jackson, and others argued strongly for deployment of ABM, for strategic reasons. Congress increased pressure on President Johnson and Secretary McNamara in the spring and summer of 1966 when both Houses approved funds for procurement of the first portion of ABM. The money had not been requested by the Johnson administration. This extraordinary action in the congressional arena brought powerful leverage to bear on the president.

At work in 1966–1967 was a loosely structured coalition of individuals and organizations, in the executive branch and in Congress, who were seeking to influence the president to deploy ABM. In addition, they were supported by influential reporters and columnists. The president also faced a potential political problem from Republican candidates for the presidency, such as Richard Nixon, who supported ABM deployment. This was a formidable array of individuals and organizations operating to deploy ABM. Their motivation was largely strategic and only marginally pork barrel.

The origins of strategic arms limitation lie in the political pressure brought to bear on Johnson and McNamara in late 1966. In an early December meeting, the JCS unanimously encouraged President Johnson to deploy ABM in an area defense. Secretary McNamara presented an alternative, suggesting that the administration "hold off spending the money [appropriated by Congress], or making a firm decision on what type of ABM system to deploy, until the State Department had explored with Moscow the idea of talks on limiting strategic arms, especially ABMs. Johnson bought the compromise, but the Joint Chiefs and other ABM adherents now felt reasonably secure that the path to deployment had been cleared."[20] The conflict between McNamara and the JCS rested on differing strategic orientations. By 1966 Secretary McNamara was increasingly unenthusiastic about the damage-limitation strategy he skillfully supported at the beginning of the Kennedy administration. The combination of endless expense, cost inefficiency, and a dangerous arms race with troubling destabilizing implications brought McNamara to oppose ABM deployment. Conversely, the JCS and other ABM supporters saw the weapon as providing a significant defensive capability against a possible Soviet nuclear attack. ABM as a defense for Minuteman missiles was of little interest to any of the services in 1966. It would not be a significant force in the debate until late in the first Nixon administration.

The Johnson administration initiated discussion with the Soviets concerning strategic arms limitation negotiations. At the Glassboro Summit in June 1967, President Johnson and Secretary McNamara explored with Premier Kosygin Soviet interest in strategic arms limitation. The Soviets, however, were not far enough along in the development of their own ABM technology to warrant hope for an immediate agreement to limit ABM deployment. The pro-ABM coalition used the budget hearings in July 1967 to force the administration to agree to deploy an ABM system against the People's Republic of China. Nevertheless, McNamara and others continued to explore strategic arms limitation negotiations with the Soviets as an alternative to ABM deployment.

Thus, the 1966–1967 ABM decision-making pattern differed strikingly from the form suggested by either the presidential or bureaucratic politics paradigms. With the electoral arena weighing heavily on Johnson's mind, two other arenas, the congressional and the public, were instrumental in the decision making. Strategic controversy between the secretary of defense and the JCS forced the issue outside the Pentagon and into the oval office. Eventually, these strategic differences forced the issue into these other arenas.

The Nixon and Ford Administrations:
Balanced Asymmetries versus Equal Aggregates

In October 1972 the Senate approved the SALT I ABM Treaty and Congress accepted the SALT I Interim Offensive Executive Agreement.[21] The ABM Treaty and Interim Offensive Agreement were qualified by the Jackson Amendment, urging the Nixon administration and the Soviet Union to quickly negotiate a permanent arms limitation treaty for offensive weapons. The amendment specified that the treaty should be based on the concept of "equal aggregates"—the United States and the Soviet Union should be limited to equal quantities of offensive weapons in all the various categories of offensive-weapon systems.

The Jackson Amendment to the SALT I agreements marked a new phase of strategic arms negotiations with the Soviet Union. The pattern of decision making would never again resemble that suggested by either the presidential politics or the bureaucratic politics paradigm. Foreign policy differences, strategic controversy, politicized procurement issues, and politicized environmental and social problems associated with strategic arms limitation turned SALT (and later START) into one of two major national security issues of the 1970s and 1980s (the other being détente). The struggle over U.S. SALT policy drove the issue from the corridors of the executive branch, to the halls of Congress, to the front pages of the nation's major newspapers, and to the board rooms of important groups seeking to lobby both the legislative and executive branches.

Two issues and a major political crisis acted as the catalysts that between 1972 and 1976 drove SALT into these other arenas. First, by 1972 considerable disenchantment was developing within the conservative community about the Nixon/Kissinger détente policy toward the Soviet Union. Second, conservatives were suspicious of the "balanced-asymmetries" approach adopted by Nixon and Kissinger for the negotiation of a permanent offensive agreement. Balanced asymmetries would except certain inequities in certain categories as long as they were balanced by Soviet inferiority in other categories. The rapid Soviet buildup in ICBMs and SLBMs (submarine-launched ballistic missiles) in the early 1970s caused the conservative community to be leery of any agreement with the Soviets without considerable U.S. strategic modernization. Finally, the Watergate crisis destroyed the credibility and authority of the Nixon administration. Nixon's political authority was so weakened that it was virtually impossible for him to control the dissidents within his own administration.

In the early 1970s Senator Henry Jackson became the spokesman for the conservative opposition. He was joined by Secretary of Defense James Schlesinger (as well as Schlesinger's successor, Donald Rumsfeld), Chief of Naval Operations Admiral Elmo R. Zumwalt, OSD representative to SALT Paul Nitze, and ACDA director Fred Iklé. An important inside player was Jackson's young aide, Richard Perle. Columnists Rowland Evans and Robert Novak were instrumental supporters of the conservative attack on détente and on the balanced-asymmetries approach to strategic arms limitation.

The conflict between these two approaches—Kissinger's détente/balanced-asymmetries approach and the conservatives' Cold War confrontationalist/equal-aggregates approach—came to a head in 1974, the year of Nixon's resignation. Kissinger and his associates in the State Department and the National Security Council staff developed the specifics of a balanced-asymmetries proposal during the winter and spring. Kissinger discussed the character of the proposal with the Soviets in Moscow in preparation for what turned out to be Richard Nixon's final summit conference with Soviet leader Leonid Brezhnev. Kissinger's approach was resisted by Schlesinger within the National Security Council meetings chaired by Nixon. Rowland and Evans attacked the balanced-asymmetries approach in the press. Jackson held hearings about the negotiation of SALT I, raising significant questions about Nixon's impending trip to Moscow and the balanced-asymmetries approach. Both Nitze and Zumwalt were significant public figures in this debate as the focus shifted from the National Security Council to the Senate and the media. By the time Nixon reached Moscow, the combination of Watergate and the conservative attack severely restricted any flexibility to negotiate on balanced asymmetries. In addition, it is improbable that the Soviets would have entertained serious compromises on SALT II given Nixon's unlikely political survival.

Negotiations with the Soviets on SALT II resumed after Nixon's resignation in August 1974. Following a Kissinger trip to Moscow in the early fall, at which time both equal aggregates and balanced asymmetries were discussed as a basis for SALT II, President Gerald Ford met with Brezhnev in November in Vladivostok to negotiate a new conceptual framework for SALT II. Ford indicates in his memoirs that the Soviets would have accepted either orientation, but that the attitude in Washington led him to propose a SALT II framework based on equal aggregates.[22]

The Vladivostok Accords had one major weakness, at least as seen by conservatives such as Senator Jackson: The Soviets retained an advantage in heavy missiles. In the months following, Jackson and other senators constrained Kissinger's efforts to turn the Vladivostok Accords into a negotiated treaty. The focus of Kissinger's and the conservatives' efforts within the executive branch, Congress, and the public arena was President Ford. In early 1976, Ford withdrew the United States from further negotiations with the Soviets about the Vladivostok Accords until after the upcoming presidential election. The Reagan attack during the presidential primary on the Nixon/ Ford détente—symbolized in the SALT II negotiations—had been the final factor in causing Ford to postpone negotiations.

Nixon and Kissinger were reluctant to build support in Congress to support their policy orientation in the face of attack from conservatives such as Senator Jackson. Given the administration's commitment to coherence, consistency, continuity, and purposive action, they were naturally inclined against involving members of Congress. Also, the Senate constituency that supported SALT was largely opposed to Nixon's political survival. Nixon and Kissinger, and later Ford, found cooperation with this group politically difficult.

The future of the SALT negotiations had become a politically important issue by 1976. There was no chance of it returning to relative invisibility in the Pentagon or elsewhere, and domestic policies were now intertwined with SALT.

The Carter Administration and SALT II:
The September Compromise

In March 1977 the secretary of state for the Carter administration, Cyrus Vance, proposed a new conceptual framework for the SALT II negotiations to the Soviets in Moscow—the "deep-cuts" concept.[23] This bold policy initiative by the new administration was meant to recapture support from both conservative and arms control groups for SALT II. No working consensus in support of SALT II had existed since the signing of the SALT I agreement. The initiative was in large part attributable to the commitment by Carter and his advisers to reassert presidential control over foreign affairs decision making and détente with the Soviet Union. When the Soviets rejected the proposal, the administration was faced with a difficult dilemma. To hang tough with the Soviets would jeopardize the support of arms controllers who believed that the Soviets would accept a modified Vladivostok Accords and that the Soviets and the United States could negotiate deeper cuts in the round of negotiations that would follow. On the other hand, to negotiate a modified Vladivostok agreement would alienate the conservatives; the administration feared confronting a hostile Senator Jackson during the treaty hearings for an agreement.

The president chose to abandon the deep cuts and seek a modified Vladivostok agreement, but one that would limit the number of warheads. The objective was to cope with the increased numbers of Soviet and U.S. warheads that resulted from the introduction of the Multiple Independently Targetable Reentry Vehicles (MIRVs), for both SLBMs and ICBMs but especially for ICBMs. These vastly increased numbers of warheads (the U.S. inventory expanded from more than 2,000 in 1972 to over 7,000 by 1977), coupled with increased accuracy, threatened the future theoretical survivability of either side's ICBM force. Of course it was the problem of U.S. ICBM survivability that captured the attention of both the public and specialists alike. Stormy controversy surrounded the issue.

The president also faced intense criticism concerning his intention to continue détente with the Soviet Union. Largely led by the Committee on the Present Danger,[24] the attack was also supported by a variety of other conservative organizations and groups, such as the American Security Council, the Coalition for Peace Through Strength, and the American Conservative Union. Most damaging was a report issued by the Senate Republicans denouncing the administration's foreign policy, especially its détente and arms control initiatives toward the Soviet Union. SALT II was taking shape in a highly charged political environment, and foreign policy sharply divided the U.S. population, especially the Carter administration and its critics.

It was in this atmosphere that the administration announced its compromise SALT II proposal. The story of the compromise with the Soviets was leaked to the press in September 1977. Conservative columns attacked the new SALT position as inferior to the deep-cuts proposal. Senator Jackson used his arms control subcommittee of the Armed Services Committee to castigate and embarrass Secretary of State Cyrus Vance and the administration. This blistering attack threatened to veto the SALT II compromise even before it was initiated as a treaty between Moscow and Washington.

The selling of the new compromise was orchestrated by a coalition of Senate aides and executive branch officers (in the executive branch, below the political appointment level). Emphasizing the introduction of warhead ceilings implicit within the agreement and the reduction of Soviet ICBM numbers, they argued that the treaty was significant in that it provided for the limitation of strategic arms and the limitation of ICBM vulnerability and thus made a modest but useful contribution to U.S. national security policy. This coalition initiated attacks in Jackson's subcommittee hearings designed to silence conservatives or at least keep them off guard. The Senate aides prepared witnesses and began subcommittee hearings of their own and, in addition, cultivated their own media support against the conservatives. Finally, they began a study group for arms control supporters, the Cranston Luncheon Group, to increase the knowledge of potential treaty supporters in the Senate and House. Later the White House would encourage and abet the Americans for SALT movement across the United States, although that movement never approached the effectiveness of the opposition's Committee on the Present Danger. Thus, by the summer of 1978 two coalitions, pro and con, vied to influence public opinion and uncommitted senators and representatives to adopt their views on the SALT II Treaty.

After Carter and Brezhnev initiated the treaty in June 1979, the political focus switched from the public and the executive branch to the Senate. The administration provided the inducements of the MX missile and an increase in military expenditures along with individual spoils to uncommitted senators in return for support of the agreement. However, in the Senate hearings the administration faced hurdles it was eventually unable to surmount. First, it could not overcome the question raised by détente, because arms control could not be disassociated from détente and because U.S.-Soviet relations deteriorated rapidly in the fall of 1979. The Cuban Brigade crisis in September, the Iranian crisis in November, and the Soviet invasion of Afghanistan in December left little that was positive in the relationship between Moscow and Washington. An arms limitation agreement between adversaries is fragile at best, but became impossible under the circumstances of early 1980. Moreover, questions of Carter's capability to lead the United States in an increasingly turbulent world, raised by his handling of the events of 1979, had a very negative impact on the treaty's reception in the Senate.

Also, verification doubts plagued the administration's effort to sell the SALT II Treaty in the Senate. Senator John Glenn, along with knowledgeable Republicans, raised serious doubts about the verifiability of the treaty until Carter withdrew it from consideration by the Senate in mid-January 1980. (The delay in the Space Shuttle program was a significant factor in this problem.)[25]

SALT II decision making during the Carter administration closely approximated the pattern of classic domestic policy decision making. Foreign policy dissension, technical problems of verification, strategic controversy, and political partisanship made strategic arms control a notorious issue that pervaded several political arenas. For the most part strategic arms limitation decision making during this period bore little resemblance to that suggested by either the bureaucratic or presidential politics paradigm.

The Reagan Administration and the MX/START Compromise

The Reagan administration was divided almost from the beginning about how to proceed with strategic arms limitation negotiations with the Soviet Union.[26] On the one hand, the faction headed by Secretary of State Alexander Haig, ACDA director Eugene Rostow, and Paul Nitze, the special ambassador to the INF (intermediate-range nuclear force) negotiations, believed that arms control with the Soviets was possible if negotiated patiently, firmly, and placed in the context of significant military modernization. Unfortunately, conflict between ACDA and the Department of State limited the cohesion of this group, and eventually, Richard Burt, director of the Bureau of Political/ Military Affairs, emerged as the leading bureaucratic player advocating this view. On the other side were Secretary of Defense Caspar Weinberger, ambassador to START General Edward Rowny, and Under Secretary of Defense Fred Iklé. Iklé's assistant, Richard Perle, assistant secretary for international security policy, emerged as the lead bureaucratic player in this group. They generally opposed arms limitation and instead sought to reassert U.S. military superiority over the Soviets.

The key to this bureaucratic struggle was President Ronald Reagan. He was generally suspicious of arms limitation negotiations, and arms limitation with the Soviet Union was even more onerous, given his dim view of that government. On the other hand, Reagan was virtually without experience in foreign affairs and was thus susceptible to arguments about the utility of arms limitation if limitation were linked to modernization of the U.S. national security forces, particularly of ICBMs. These contradictory impulses resulted in ambiguity, and even occasional disinterest, on the part of the president as to whether or not the United States should take an active role in START.

The bureaucratic forces opposed to serious arms limitation negotiations proved to be more influential in the first two years of the administration. As a result, U.S. policy seemed to be more interested in scoring debating points than exploring effective arms limitation with the Soviets. The stalemate in START was reinforced by the disintegrating political environment between the superpowers. In 1983, two factors combined to alter the president's attitude toward strategic arms limitation with the Soviet Union. First, the Reagan administration had experienced two very significant reversals in its strategic modernization program. In October 1981, President Reagan rejected the Carter proposal to place MX in multiple protective shelters (MPS) in the Nevada and Utah Great Basin. He proposed instead an interim solution—to deploy MX in Minuteman silos while exploring several long-term deployment modes. The president's proposal was not supported in the air force, the Senate Armed Services Committee, and in Congress—all three of which had previously been generally supportive of the idea of a new ICBM. In fact, this alternative had already been proposed and rejected by Congress in the last year of the Ford administration.

In January, the Reagan administration withdrew the interim proposal and promised to provide a long-term solution by the end of the year. In December 1982, the administration proposed the "closely spaced basing" mode or, as it was more commonly known, "dense pack." Within days this was rejected, literally without a hearing. The administration had suffered two defeats of its proposed basing modes after rejecting what was perhaps the most survivable concept (MX-MPS). It was on the verge of seeing the centerpiece of its strategic modernization program, the MX, abandoned by Congress as unworkable.

MX was important to both the Burt and Perle factions within the administration. For the Burt group, if serious negotiations were to proceed, the Soviets had to understand that the United States was serious about strategic modernization; obviously, such an impression would not be conveyed if the administration was unable to deploy MX. From the Perle faction's point of view, if U.S. military superiority was to be reestablished, MX had to be deployed. By January 1983 the administration was in jeopardy of losing on both counts.

The second factor in altering the president's attitude was the dramatic intensification of U.S. public support of strategic arms limitation. In 1983 the nuclear freeze movement had become a powerful force in U.S. politics. Senators and representatives were barraged by letters, phone calls, and visits from constituents urging them to vote for mutual freeze in the deployment of nuclear weapons. Most strategic specialists within the administration saw the freeze movement as a dangerous intrusion into the field of executive branch responsibility for foreign policy. Moreover, it was increasingly apparent that if the administration did not become more serious about strategic arms limitation with the Soviet Union, the movement might force upon the administration some type of freeze in the deployment of nuclear weapons.

Opponents of the Weinberger-Perle coalition both within the administration and outside it (but especially outside it), believed that an opportunity now existed to forcefully alter the malaise in national security policy that had existed for the past several years. Such a change would necessitate integrating MX, strategic doctrine, and strategic arms limitation under a common national security policy. They decided to develop a coalition of individuals and organizations whose task it would be to alter the administration's emphasis on fighting and winning a nuclear war, to support the deployment of MX, and to initiate serious strategic arms limitation negotiations with the Soviet Union. Retired General Brent Scowcroft, who with his staff was a member of this coalition, was asked by Reagan to head a presidential commission review of the administration's strategic policy, with special emphasis on recommending a basing mode that would be acceptable to the Congress. In fact, the commission was asked to establish a base of support within the Congress for the recommended mode. Between January and the fall of 1983, General Scowcroft and his associates worked hard to establish a new strategic policy for the Reagan administration, a new rationale for MX along with an acceptable basing mode, a realistic position for the START negotiations, and a base of political support for these initiatives.

This coalition of executive branch officials, quasi–executive branch personnel (for example, Scowcroft), members of Congress (for example, Representative Les Aspin), and media individuals were opposed by the Perle group within the administration as well as by a loosely related but significant group of MX opponents in the House and the media. Strategic arms limitation and MX procurement policy decision making was reduced to coalition conflict, operating in several political arenas during 1983. The decision making certainly did not resemble that described and predicted by either the bureaucratic or presidential politics paradigm.

CONCLUSIONS

By examining several of the SALT and START episodes over the past eighteen years, it is clear that several factors drove strategic arms limitation decision making out of the traditional narrow confines of the executive branch into a pattern that more closely resembles domestic policy decision making. These factors were: presidential disinterest and vagueness; strategic dissension; technical and verification problems; foreign policy linkage; association with procurement issues; and politicized environmental/social/financial difficulties. The bureaucratic and presidential politics paradigms explain only two of the six episodes of U.S. strategic arms limitation decision making: During the first Nixon administration U.S. decision making resembled the presidential politics paradigm; in the Johnson administration between 1967 and 1968 the strategic arms limitation decision making resembled the bureaucratic politics paradigm. Thus, both paradigms were deficient in describing, let alone explaining and predicting, U.S. strategic arms limitation decision making.

In determining the character of the decision making in each episode, two critical factors were the role of the president and the visibility of the issue. During his first administration, President Nixon was strong and determined enough to control the executive branch decision making for SALT. Moreover, the circumstances of that period combined to divert general attention from SALT to other foreign policy issues. In the second episode, President Johnson delegated decision making for SALT to the interested executive branch agencies. In addition, SALT decision making was virtually invisible in U.S. politics between 1967 and 1968. The combination of the role of the president and the low profile of the SALT issue was critical to the pattern of decision making.

In the other four episodes, both the role of the president and the visibility of the strategic arms limitation issue were very much different from that in these first two cases. Presidents Johnson, Nixon, Ford, Carter, and Reagan neither controlled the executive branch decision making, as the president did in the first two cases, nor was the issue as invisible. On the contrary, these presidents (for differing reasons) were either not committed to strategic arms limitation or were not strong enough to control the decision making within the executive branch, or both. As a result, the decision making spilled over into the congressional and public arenas as contending parties in the debate about SALT sought to develop influential allies to effect strategic arms limitation decision making.

Moreover, strategic dissension within these administrations over SALT and START policy became exacerbated when linked to strategic policy, verification problems, détente and U.S.-Soviet relations, questions of procurement of strategic weapons (especially MX), and the politicized environment in which SALT and START were considered by the public and Congress. All this made strategic arms limitation policy the most visible foreign policy issue of the 1970s and first part of the 1980s. The visibility and intensity of the issue made it impossible to handle SALT or START in a decision-making pattern similar to either the bureaucratic or presidential politics paradigm, even if the presidents in these four episodes had been committed and powerful enough to control decision making within their administrations.

It is unlikely that the strategic arms limitation issue will recede into the background in the future. The saliency of the nuclear issue to the U.S. public and the world prevents its return to the relative invisibility of the late 1960s and early 1970s. Moreover, the strategic arms limitation issue is intimately related to other issues—such as détente, strategic policy, and the nuclear freeze movement—that further divide the political environment.

As a consequence of the altered decision-making environment, if the United States is to effectively pursue strategic arms limitation, it must be clearly understood that emphasis on executive branch or congressional branch prerogative in decision making is not enough. A president must be committed to strategic arms limitation and organize the executive branch in such a way as to force a rationale on the negotiations. But more important, the president and others in Congress and the public arenas must actively forge a consensus in support of the U.S. negotiating position. Coherence, consistency, continuity, and purposive action in strategic arms limitation negotiations is the objective for which governments should strive. But these qualities require leadership—vision, commitment, and political skills to mobilize support—in both the executive branch and the Congress. Such a situation more closely resembles the pattern of decision making of the Reagan administration's 1981 governmental and tax revolution than it does the SALT initiatives of either 1967–1968 or 1969–1973. The Reagan administration will have to reassert that pattern in START if it is to successfully negotiate an arms limitation or reduction agreement between the United States and the Soviet Union.

NOTES

1. See, for example, Thomas Schelling and Morton Halperin, *Strategy and Arms Control* (New York: Twentieth Century Fund, 1961); Thomas Schelling, *Arms and Influence* (New Haven, Conn.: Yale University Press, 1966); Donald G. Brennan, *Arms Control, Disarmament, and National Security* (New York: George Braziller, 1961); Bernard S. Brodie, *Strategy in the Missile Age* (Princeton, N.J.: Princeton University Press, 1959); Hedley Bull, *The Control of the Arms Race* (New York: Frederick A. Praeger, 1961); Herman Kahn, *On Thermonuclear War* (Princeton, N.J.: Princeton University Press, 1960); and Herman Kahn, *On Escalation* (New York: Frederick A. Praeger, 1965).

2. See Charles McClelland, "The Acute International Crisis," *World Politics* 14 (October 1961):182–204; A. J. Wiener and Herman Kahn, eds., *Crisis and Arms Control* (New York: Hudson Institute, 1962); Albert Wohlstetter and Roberta Wohlstetter, *Controlling the Risks in Cuba,* Adelphi Paper no. 17 (London: The International Institute for Strategic Studies, 1965); Oran R. Young, *The Intermediaries: Third Parties in International Crisis* (Princeton, N.J.: Princeton University Press, 1967); Charles F. Hermann, "International Crisis as a Situational Variable," in James N. Rosenau, ed., *International Politics and Foreign Policy* (New York: Free Press, 1969); George W. Rathjens, "The Dynamics of the Arms Race," *Scientific American* 221 (April 1969); Colin Gray, "The Arms Race Phenomenon," *World Politics* 24 (October 1971); Colin Gray, "The Urge To Compete," *World Politics* 26 (January 1974):207–233; Graham T. Allison, "Questions About the Arms Race: Who's Racing Whom? A Bureaucratic Perspective," in Robert Pfaltzgraff, Jr., ed., *Contrasting Approaches to Strategic Arms Control* (Lexington, Mass.: Lexington Books, 1974); Graham T. Allison and Frederic A. Morris, "Armaments and Arms Control: Exploring Determinants," in Franklin A. Long and George W. Rathjens, eds., *Defense Policy and Arms Control* (New York: W. W. Norton and Company, 1965); and Ralph Lapp, *Arms Beyond Doubt: The Tyranny of Weapons Technology* (New York: Cowles, 1970).

3. Lauren H. Holland and Robert A. Hoover, *The MX Decision: A New Direction in U.S. Weapons Procurement Policy?* (Boulder, Colo.: Westview Press, 1985).

4. For a discussion of the presidential politics paradigm, see Alexander L. George, *Presidential Decisionmaking in Foreign Policy: The Effective Use of Information and Advice* (Boulder, Colo.: Westview Press, 1980).

5. See, for example, the more important contributions to the general bureaucratic politics paradigm literature: Samuel P. Huntington, *The Common Defense* (New York: Columbia University Press, 1961); Graham T. Allison, "Conceptual Models and the Cuban Missile Crisis," *American Political Science Review* 43 (September 1969); Graham T. Allison, *Essence of Decision: Explaining the Cuban Missile Crisis* (Boston: Little, Brown and Company, 1971); Graham T. Allison and Morton Halperin, "Bureaucratic Politics: A Paradigm and Some Policy Implications," in Raymond Tanter and Richard H. Ullman, eds., *Theory and Policy in International Relations* (Princeton, N.J.: Princeton University Press, 1972); Morton Halperin and Arnold Kanter, *Readings in American Foreign Policy: A Bureaucratic Perspective* (Boston: Little, Brown and Company, 1973); and Morton Halperin, *Bureaucratic Politics and Foreign Policy* (Washington, D.C.:

Brookings Institution, 1974). For a review of the literature as well as a criticism of the bureaucratic politics paradigm literature, see Dan Caldwell, "Bureaucratic Foreign Policy-Making," *American Behavioral Scientist* 21 (September/October 1977).

6. Holland and Hoover, *The MX Decision*, p. 1.

7. Caldwell, "Bureaucratic Foreign Policy-Making," p. 88.

8. See note 5, above.

9. The discussion of the propositions of the bureaucratic politics paradigm draws on two works by Lauren H. Holland and Robert A. Hoover: *The MX Decision* and "Defense Policymaking Unmasked: Three Recent Cases of Weapons Procurement," in Joseph R. Goldman, ed., *Issues and Choices* (Lexington: University of Kentucky Press, 1985).

10. Stephen D. Krasner, "Are Bureaucracies Important? (Or Allison Wonderland)," *Foreign Policy* 7 (Summer 1972).

11. Caldwell, "Bureaucratic Foreign Policy-Making."

12. The discussion of the propositions of the presidential politics paradigm draws on the analysis of Robert A. Hoover, "Strategic Arms Limitation, the Presidency and Congress," Paper presented at the annual International Studies Association meeting, March 1980, Los Angeles, Calif. In that manuscript both the executive/legislative politics and the coalition politics paradigms are analyzed.

13. The discussion of the first episode draws largely on Henry Kissinger, *The White House Years* (Boston: Little, Brown and Company, 1979); Gerard Smith, *Doubletalk: The Story of SALT I* (New York: Doubleday, 1980); John Newhouse, *Cold Dawn: The Story of SALT* (New York: Holt, Rinehart, and Winston, 1973); and Alan Platt, *The U.S. Senate and Strategic Arms Policy, 1969–1977* (Boulder, Colo.: Westview Press, 1978).

14. Seymour M. Hersh, *The Price of Power: Kissinger in the Nixon White House* (New York: Summit Books, 1983), pp. 380, 400, 465–474, 476–477.

15. Smith, *Doubletalk*, pp. 241–242.

16. Kissinger, *The White House Years*, pp. 226–312.

17. The discussion of the second episode is based on Morton Halperin, "The Decision to Deploy the ABM: Bureaucratic and Domestic Politics in the Johnson Administration," *World Politics* 25 (October 1972):62–95; Halperin, *Bureaucratic Politics and Foreign Policy;* Newhouse, *Cold Dawn;* James Kurth, "A Widening Gyre: The Logic of American Weapons Procurement," *Public Policy* 7 (Summer 1971):373–404; and Ernest J. Yanarella, *The Missile Defense Controversy: Strategy, Technology, and Politics, 1955–1972* (Lexington: University of Kentucky Press, 1977).

18. The discussion of the third episode is drawn from Halperin, "The Decision to Deploy the ABM"; Newhouse, *Cold Dawn;* and Yanarella, *The Missile Defense Controversy.*

19. Halperin, "The Decision to Deploy the ABM," p. 63.

20. Newhouse, *Cold Dawn*, p. 86.

21. The discussion of the fourth episode draws largely on Kissinger, *The White House Years;* Peter J. Ognibene, *Scoop: The Life and Politics of Henry M. Jackson* (New York: Stein and Day, 1975); Platt, *The U.S. Senate and Strategic Arms Policy, 1969–1977;* and Elmo R. Zumwalt, *On Watch* (New York: Quadrangle, 1976).

22. Gerald R. Ford, *A Time to Heal: The Autobiography of Gerald R. Ford* (New York: Harper and Row, 1979), pp. 214–215.

23. The discussion of the fifth episode is based on Strobe Talbott, *Endgame: The Inside Story of SALT I* (New York: Harper and Row, 1979); Zbigniew Brzezinski, *Power and Principle* (New York: Farrar, Straus and Giroux, 1983); and Cyrus Vance, *Hard Choices: Critical Years in America's Foreign Policy* (New York: Simon and

Schuster, 1983). It is also drawn from forty-four confidential interviews that I conducted between 1978 and 1982, with members of Congress, the Carter executive branch, and critics of the administration. Research for this project was supported by a grant from the College of Humanities, Arts and Social Sciences of Utah State University during 1980.

24. The Committee on the Present Danger, which became an active and forceful critic of Carter's SALT II policy, included such prominent conservatives as Ronald Reagan, Richard Allen, James Buckley, W. Glenn Campbell, William Casey, John Connally, John Foster, Jr., Fred Charles Iklé, Jeane Kirkpatrick, John Lehman, Clare Booth Luce, Paul Nitze, Edward Noble, Richard Perle, Eugene Rostow, Richard Pipes, Paul Seabury, Edward Bennett Williams, and Seymour Weiss (Ronald Brownstein and Nini Easton, *Reagan's Ruling Class* [New York: Pantheon, 1983], pp. 533–534). For a discussion of the development of the Committee on the Present Danger, see Jerry Sanders, *Peddlers of Crisis: The Committee on the Present Danger and the Politics of Containment* (New York: South End Press, 1983).

25. Author's interviews (see note 23).

26. The discussion of the sixth episode is based on Strobe Talbott, *Deadly Gambits: The Reagan Administration and the Stalemate in Nuclear Arms Control* (New York: Knopf, 1984); Elizabeth Drew, "A Political Journal," *New Yorker* 59 (20 June 1983):39–75; and Holland and Hoover, *The MX Decision.*

7

TECHNOLOGICAL DEVELOPMENT, THE MILITARY BALANCE, AND ARMS CONTROL

KURT GOTTFRIED

TRINITY

Just forty years ago, as dawn broke over the New Mexico desert, the first nuclear explosion was detonated. The energy released equaled that available from some 20,000 tons of TNT—20 kilotons. Within the month Hiroshima and Nagasaki lay in ruins. These events occurred just six years after the discovery of nuclear fission in 1939. In the time that many talented individuals need to earn their doctorate degrees, a two-man table-top experiment at the outer frontier of an arcane science had been transformed into history's most spectacular breakthrough in military technology.[1]

A variety of circumstances combined to make this revolution possible. First, the new field of nuclear physics was being explored by an exceptionally brilliant group of scientists. By 1939 this branch of physics had reached a level of precocious sophistication in which ingenious breakthroughs had become almost routine. Second, many outstanding members of this international scientific fraternity had fled Nazi Germany and settled in the United States. And third, their new home was remarkably open to newcomers, disposed of vast resources, and had repeatedly demonstrated a genius for organizing technological enterprises on a momentous scale. The Manhattan Project displayed all these U.S. strengths in spades.

In the aftermath of the bombing of Hiroshima many Americans naturally felt confident that they would enjoy complete security into the distant future. Their homeland's great oceanic barriers were buttressed by a weapon of demonic power that exploited a sophisticated technology that no potential adversary could match. But this view was not shared by the senior Manhattan Project scientists. They were aware that the basic principles behind the bomb would be obvious to the brilliant Russian physicists they knew personally, and who they predicted could develop a nuclear bomb for the Soviet Union within five years. To a layperson this expectation was surprising. Russia had just been devastated by war, and its prewar technology and industry had been primitive in comparison to that of the United States. Nevertheless, this forecast proved to be correct; the first successful Soviet bomb test occurred in 1949.

There is little question that the physicist-spy Klaus Fuchs contributed to the speed with which the Soviets accomplished this feat. But it is also true that the Soviets had already embarked on the quest for a nuclear bomb on their own initiative.[2] An outstanding Leningrad physicist, Igor Kurchatov, recognized the military potential of nuclear fission from the start. In a remarkable illustration of what the term "intelligence" can mean, one of Kurchatov's young associates, G. N. Flyorov, deduced the existence of a U.S. bomb project when, on a visit to a provincial library while on leave from the front, he noticed that in the *Physical Review* there were no longer any articles on nuclear physics by the habitually prolific physicists of the United States. Flyorov wrote directly to Stalin, and his unlikely information gave partial impetus to the Soviet effort to develop a nuclear bomb, so that the Soviets were on their way when the facility at Los Alamos was established. All this does not mean that Soviet scientists had given their nation a nuclear arsenal that by 1950 matched ours. Indeed, the Soviet Union did not reach "strategic parity" until the mid-1970s. But by the early 1960s the Soviets had acquired a credible deterrent. As former Secretary of Defense Robert McNamara said, "Number one, I didn't believe, and President Kennedy didn't believe, we had a first-strike capability; number two, we didn't have any intention of trying to attain a first-strike capability. Number three, if we had had any such intention, there is no way we could have done it, in my opinion."[3]

What are we to infer from this tale? Some believe that the United States sat on its laurels and did not exploit its lead out of the starting gate with enough zeal and tenacity. Perhaps. But that opinion ignores all the U.S. "firsts" of the period from 1945 to 1960—the intercontinental bomber, the hydrogen bomb, the photographic surveillance satellite, and the submarine-launched missile—and it also forgets that the U.S. ICBM (intercontinental ballistic missile) buildup during the

1960s was far swifter than the Soviet ICBM buildup. As for the more recent past, this view discounts the fact that multiple-warhead missiles (MIRVs—multiple independently targetable reentry vehicles), high-accuracy inertial guidance for ICBMs, and high-accuracy air-launched cruise missiles, now deployed on U.S. bombers, were all U.S. innovations. Almost all new technologies of relevance to the nuclear strategic forces first arrived on the scene adorned with stars and stripes, whereas their hammer-and-sickle counterparts followed some five years later on average. So U.S. sloth does not account for the Soviets' ability to threaten the survival of the United States.

The explanation for the strength of Soviet nuclear capability is to be found elsewhere—in the truly revolutionary nature of the technologies of thermonuclear explosives and intercontinental ballistic missiles. Once a nation with the human and material resources of the Soviet Union (or, for that matter, France or Great Britain) acquires the ability to mass-produce weapons based on those technologies, it can wreak unacceptable damage on any would-be aggressor, no matter how strong the aggressor may be.

NUCLEAR SCHIZOPHRENIA AND NUCLEAR SANITY

The nuclear-arms race stems from a variety of causes. Suspicion, fear, animosity, ambition, and technological hubris have all contributed. But there is also a conceptual cause: a persistent inability to decide whether or not nuclear explosives are weapons. Some of the policies and actions of the superpowers are based on the thesis that nuclear warheads are not weapons in the traditional sense; that they only serve to deter the use of such devices by the adversary. Other policies and actions are only credible if these same devices are intended to play the traditional roles of weapons—as tools for attaining a finite and reasonably well defined political or military objective.

Examples that illustrate this international case of schizophrenia abound. Much of what we hear seems to say, either out loud or by implication, that the advent of nuclear explosives has not altered the age-old meanings of certain words. "War," "weapon," and "defense" retain their venerable significance in our understanding of the relentless quest for more accurate and flexible means of nuclear-weapons delivery; of the installation of missile defenses around Moscow; or in the more modest rationales put forward in support of the Strategic Defense Initiative (SDI). The traditional meanings of these words figure in the planning and routine training for nuclear operations by North Atlantic Treaty Organization (NATO) and Warsaw Pact armies, as well as in those military doctrines that either hope or assume that nuclear war can be controlled and that are then used to assess and to justify nuclear-weapons requirements by both superpowers.[4]

In contrast, another array of facts, attitudes, policies, and actions implies that the meanings of "war," "weapon," and "defense" have changed drastically. Much of arms control seeks to impede the development of "better" nuclear weapons and of defenses against them, and on occasion these efforts have actually succeeded. The most important illustration of this novel facet of international relations is the Anti-Ballistic Missile (ABM) Treaty of 1972, which originated in response to the deployment of an ABM system at Moscow. This treaty places strict constraints not only on deployment but even on research and development of missile defenses, a notion that a pre-Hiroshima soldier or statesman would find both bizarre and immoral. The plans and preparations for using nuclear explosives on potential European battlefields have been overseen by many military and civilian leaders who have, on leaving office, made no secret of their concern (and sometimes even of their conviction) that such use would lead to the destruction of Europe and to uncontrollable escalation.[5]

For that matter, many Western European leaders believe that the defense of their own nations ultimately rests on the assurance that the Soviet Union and the United States would both be devastated should there be a Soviet incursion across the East-West border. In the Pentagon the civilian leadership has at various times been captivated by sophisticated strategies for prosecuting controlled intercontinental nuclear wars, but these same leadership groups have usually been reluctant to allocate enough resources to the command and control systems that are needed to execute the far simpler strategy of assured retaliation that they decry.[6] And President Reagan, in calling for a defense that would make nuclear weapons "impotent and obsolete," has in effect said that his nuclear arsenal threatens to stimulate the destruction of the nation that it is supposed to protect. Surely that is a clear signal that Reagan does not believe that nuclear explosives serve the traditional purpose of weapons.

It is not possible to construct a sound defense policy by evading these dilemmas concerning the nature and role of nuclear explosives. The problem of defense against nuclear attack offers the best insight into this problem. When a single attack could only destroy a small portion of an enemy's resources, defense relied either on destruction of the attacker or on attrition. For example, the Nazis had to abandon their plan to invade Britain because the Royal Air Force, with the help of newly invented radar, was able to attain a 10 percent attrition rate against German bombers. Against such odds it was too costly to sustain the repeated attacks that German military objectives required. A single nuclear attack, on the other hand, can spell total disaster, so attrition is not an option available to the defense. Furthermore, there still exists no known combination of techniques that can fully repel an airborne attack. The Soviet Union has deployed well over 10,000 surface-to-air missiles in addition to a vast fleet of fighter planes, and yet the U.S. air force claims, and independent analysts agree, that U.S. manned bombers could penetrate those defenses and drop nuclear weapons on Soviet targets. (Those bombers can also remain outside Soviet airspace and launch highly accurate nuclear-armed cruise missiles against targets deep inside the Soviet Union.)

Given that manned bombers are far slower and larger than missile boosters, and that bombers (and cruise missiles) are also much more fragile than missile warheads, we can readily see that a highly proficient defense against a large attack by nuclear-armed missiles is a formidable task at best. A large missile attack could easily contain thousands of thermonuclear warheads, each far more destructive than the fission weapons that destroyed Hiroshima and Nagasaki, and a successful defense of cities against such an attack would therefore have to perform with an attrition rate bordering on 100 percent. Until such a prodigious attrition rate is within reach, only highly resilient and expendable targets could be defended. Nothing but hardened missile silos and their launch control facilities answer to this description, because they could survive anything short of a near hit, and they are also so numerous that each superpower would retain a viable deterrent force even if it were to lose the bulk of its land-based missiles.[7]

Fleets of nuclear-armed missiles are really something quite new in the military lexicon. They can destroy a world power on demand; no defense of populations against such an attack is in sight; and the nation that perpetrates such an attack would almost certainly be committing suicide, no matter how clever its military plans, as its victim could launch a counterattack before the original attack struck home.[8] Furthermore, there is a widespread consensus that any use of nuclear weapons in field warfare poses a serious risk of escalation to intercontinental strategic exchanges; indeed, many Western military leaders believe that such an outcome would be the most likely consequence of nuclear warfare, and what is known from Soviet military writings lends strong support to such fears. The proverbial "prudent military planner" should therefore conclude that any and all nuclear-armed devices are not weapons, but only serve to deter a potential adversary from using his own nuclear "weapons."

For that matter, prudence would indicate that even direct non-nuclear conflict between the superpowers, especially in a theater of great value to both of them, would carry with it a large risk of escalation across the nuclear threshold and into the forbidden region of strategic exchange. We may take comfort from the observation that when faced with the prospect of actual confrontation both sides usually recognize the validity of this judgment.[9] On the other hand, the policies that guide their strategic weapons programs seem to be oblivious to that commonsense judgment.

TECHNOLOGICAL INNOVATION AND RESTRAINT

If we accept the proposition that nuclear weapons only serve to deter,[10] we may ask what principles should govern our policies regarding military technology. This is a complex question. Among other things, the answers clearly depend on the level of cooperation that the superpowers can achieve despite their geopolitical competition. Technical innovations can exacerbate or alleviate the hazards of that competition. Technologies that aggravate the political situation are too familiar to require any comment. A benign example is a satellite that carries instruments that can detect the heat (infrared) radiation from a rocket's exhaust plume and thus provides early warning of missile launches. In peacetime such satellites give each side continuous assurance that no attack is at hand.[11] Some technologies are two-faced; whether they are benign or not depends on the political environment. Photo-reconnaissance satellites have this character: In peacetime they are essential to treaty verification, but in wartime the information that they patiently collected over the years would be used to accurately aim missiles of every variety.[12]

These examples demonstrate that in discussing technological innovation we shall have to define the political setting in which they take place, as well as the political relationships technology should seek to foster. Our discussion will be based on two premises: (1) The security of one superpower cannot be improved by technological innovations that enhance the threat to the other's existence; and (2) no law of man or nature stipulates that technology is unrestrainable.

The first premise is the lesson of post-1945 history, but the second is open to serious doubt. Technological restraint runs counter to the American grain and to a deep current in Western thought and culture. Many believe that those who ask for such restraints are aping King Canute's command that the tide should stop rising. This belief is widely held by scientists and engineers, who have been eyewitnesses to technical revolutions that most of them were unable to foresee.

Every high-energy physicist at work in an accelerator that is miles across knows that some fifty years ago the first cyclotron could be held in one of Ernest Lawrence's hands. Today's personal computer is more powerful and vastly more reliable than the front-line computers that filled whole buildings thirty years ago. Similar comparisons describe military technology: The Hiroshima weapon was barely able to fit into the bomber from which it was dropped, whereas today's far more powerful missile warhead is several feet long and can hit a target continents away with an accuracy measured in hundreds of yards. Why should anyone hope that such developments can be impeded?

Before accepting this fatalistic appraisal, we should recognize that the preceding paragraph lumps activities that are actually quite different—research, development, and deployment—and does not differentiate between technological innovation that incurs no hostile response from an adversary and that which does. In the world of *Realpolitik* the only restraint on laboratory research and development can come from the independent decisions of sovereign nations based on the priorities set by their own political processes. But once we leave the laboratory for activities on a scale that may be visible from afar, constraints that do not depend on good faith become possible provided two conditions are attainable: that both superpowers perceive restraint to be in their national interest; and that they believe that they are able to adequately verify compliance with the constraint in question. Whether the international agreement that underlies such an arrangement is codified in a formal treaty or is merely a tacit understanding is not of fundamental importance, as there is no police force that can incarcerate a nation that violates international legal obligations. If either superpower were to decide that the activities of the other threatened its vital interests, it would act to protect itself even if those activities complied with formal or tacit understandings.[13]

The question of verification is certainly a greater problem for the United States than it is for the Soviet Union. With but rare exceptions, the Soviets do not express concern about their ability to adequately monitor U.S. defense activities. Just the need of the U.S. government to obtain congressional approval for military funding provides mountains of prior evidence, to which are added the investigative skills of the Western press and academic communities, not to mention outright espionage. But all this should not mislead us into believing that, by contrast, the Soviet Union is still "a riddle wrapped in a mystery inside an enigma." Thanks in large measure to technology, the West has acquired an ever more accurate picture of Soviet military activities.[14] Sensors in space, on the earth's surface, and on airplanes listen to a vast range of signals that the Soviets must use in their day-to-day activities, and it is not yet possible to encrypt more than a small portion of this message traffic. Satellites capture detailed images of the Soviet Union, both in the visible and the invisible portions of the spectrum; radars and optical instruments watch all Soviet space activities; submarines and surface vessels gather a wide variety of data. In addition, human intelligence is important, especially in the case of strategic weapons development, in which many years separate deployment from original blueprint so that even a low rate of information leakage can become highly significant. In any event, despite the Soviet obsession with secrecy, such authorities as former CIA director William F. Colby have stated that the United States has always anticipated what the characteristics of major Soviet strategic weapons would be prior to their deployment.[15] Some inkling can be gained of what is known to the U.S. government from the portion of these data available in the open literature, which describes not only Soviet weapon systems but also Soviet military training and operational procedures.[16]

The so-called national technical means for verification available to the United States are formidable and continually improving, but their limits must be understood in considering any particular constraint on development or deployment. Furthermore, several generic features of verification are frequently misunderstood. First, monitoring another nation's activities is, in essence, a statistical process; there is always some probability that any particular action will not be seen or will be misinterpreted. Second, in assessing the value of any constraint, the risk that some forbidden activity is not apprehended must be balanced against the risks that an unconstrained regime would entail. Both of these features are familiar in everyday life. If we run a red light or go the wrong way on a one-way street there is some probability that we will not be caught. Hence "verification" of traffic laws is imperfect, but we accept imperfection in comparison to anarchy, which would force us to travel about in armored vehicles.[17] Because of this statistical character of verification, it is relatively straightforward to reliably monitor compliance with numerical limits on large deployments of big objects, such as strategic bombers, ICBMs, or missile submarines. Verification of agreements that specify the characteristics of these weapons is, of course, harder, but the slow pace of development, the lengthy teething process, and the very size of the strategic forces all combine to make the inevitable uncertainties in such verification relatively insignificant.

A much more intricate situation is exemplified by proposals that would forbid the testing of antisatellite (ASAT) weapons.[18] Military satellites are relatively few in number, and the loss of even a handful could be very significant. As a consequence, even a limited ASAT capability might be deemed intolerable. The Soviet Union has tested an orbiting ASAT weapon with a moderate level of success; the United States is about to begin the testing of a far more sophisticated and nimble ASAT that would be launched at high altitude from a jet fighter. Is it then in the U.S. national interest to agree to a ban on further tests of space weapons that, among other things, would prevent further tests of its new ASAT? Many factors must be weighed in striking this balance: Is the United States more or less dependent on military satellites than the Soviet Union? How significant a military threat does the Soviet ASAT pose? Would a U.S. ASAT deter the Soviets from using their ASAT? Could the Soviets develop a better ASAT system clandestinely under the nose of U.S. space surveillance systems? Because existing weapons, such as ICBMs and manned maneuvering spacecraft, could be used to destroy or damage satellites, is there any utility in a restraint on ASAT development? Given this long list of questions, and the multiplicity of further questions that each leads to, it should come as no surprise that there is a spectrum of opinion concerning the feasibility and significance of an ASAT test ban treaty and that the differing viewpoints are ultimately based on rather broad considerations.

For example, supporters of SDI are opposed to ASAT constraints because virtually every ballistic missile interceptor is automatically an ASAT. Others believe that the first priority should be the protection of high-altitude (geosynchronous) satellites, as they are vital to the strategic command and control systems, and that it is already too late to ban ASATs because such a ban would threaten reconnaissance satellites operating at lower altitudes. I propose a third view: Although perfect protection against low-altitude satellites is not attainable, it is nonetheless important to prevent the deployment of ASATs that could swiftly and confidently eliminate whole constellations of such satellites. This conclusion rests on the following considerations: (1) U.S. ability to monitor Soviet space activities would, with good confidence, prevent the development of a highly capable ASAT, together with its elaborate ground-control facilities, because the Soviet military would not rely on such a complex system without elaborate tests;[19] (2) the threat from the existing Soviet ASAT, and other Soviet space activities, could be offset by providing our satellites with on-board threat assessment equipment and more maneuverability and by deploying spare satellites in orbit or ready for launch; (3) it is, above all, important to prevent the deployment of highly capable ASATs that could quickly destroy whole sets of low-orbit satellites because such ASAT attacks in a crisis or low-level conflict could stimulate escalation; and (4) in the absence of a ban on low-orbit ASATs, beam weapons on low-orbit space platforms could be developed that could eventually be turned upward against the distant and vital geosynchronous satellites and thereby trigger a strategic confrontation.

The ASAT problem illustrates the complex factors that must often be weighed in placing constraints on military technology. Nevertheless, two lessons may be drawn from this example. First, in the last analysis, broad considerations that go far beyond the specific military technology usually dominate; and second, if the constraint in question is believed to be desirable, technology itself can often provide essential support for that constraint. Thus, a government that desires an ASAT constraint, but is concerned about its ability to verify an ASAT test ban, could opt to devote resources to enhance that ability. The technologies that are being developed for SDI have a mission that is far more demanding than what would be needed to verify an ASAT test ban. The systems required by SDI must be able to track and identify large numbers of space objects, assign them to interceptors, and assess damage, all in a matter of, at most, minutes. By contrast, an ASAT test ban surveillance system must only watch a small set of isolated events and analyze them at a leisurely pace with the help of humans. In addition to better monitoring, technology can provide protection against the contingency that the adversary is cheating. We already discussed the measures that could be taken to protect satellites. A complementary but quite different form of protection would be provided by a research program into ASAT techniques that complied with the treaty constraints, but that would allow one side to move efficiently toward ASAT deployment should the other side violate the agreement. Indeed, such a research program is a deterrent to such an action.

There are other areas in which technological innovation can support a hard-nosed but truly defensive security posture. This discussion of the possibilities of ASAT arms control actually applies almost verbatim to constraints on ballistic missile research.[20] Great ingenuity has already been devoted to developing unmanned devices for on-site inspection of a treaty that would ban all underground tests of nuclear weapons.[21] Perhaps the most critical area for benign technical innovation is in command and control.[22] It is essential for crisis management that strategic forces be under the control of a highly robust and reliable system that promptly provides civilian and military leaders with secure and understandable data concerning the status of their own forces and those of a potential adversary.

SCIENTIFIC ADVICE AND RESPONSIBILITY

That twentieth-century science has transformed the military and political landscape is recognized by one and all. Nevertheless, in the United States scientific advice to the government has been a remarkably haphazard affair. The President's Science Advisory Committee (PSAC) existed for only fifteen of the forty years since Hiroshima, from 1957 to 1972. Initiated at the same time as the position of science adviser, during the second Eisenhower administration, the committee played a significant role in a number of national decisions related to constraints on strategic forces, especially those concerning nuclear tests in the atmosphere and missile defenses, both of which are embodied in ratified treaties. The PSAC was composed of very prominent scientists who were neither government employees nor, in general, employees of defense contractors and whose appointments were not correlated to presidential elections. It was a body that, through the science adviser, could offer expert and independent advice that was relatively uncontaminated by personal considerations or political bias.[23] The entire science advisory apparatus was disbanded by President Richard Nixon after it had disagreed with his administration's position on the merits of an ABM system and the supersonic transport (SST). Although the office of science adviser was subsequently reestablished, that post has never regained the status that it had when it was backed by a committee with the standing of the PSAC.

The absence of a highly qualified, independent, and influential science advisory organization was apparent in the manner in which the Strategic Defense Initiative was launched. Whatever we may think of it, President Reagan's initiative is a truly important turning point in the strategic confrontation. It is therefore astonishing, but none-theless true, that the technical merits of SDI were studied by advisory panels only after the famous speech of 23 March 1983. For that matter, it is also abundantly clear from their prior and subsequent testimony, that the most senior technical officials in the Pentagon (in particular, the deputy secretary of defense for research and engineering and the director of the Defense Advanced Research Agency) were not consulted by the White House. Given the president's evident and deep personal commitment to the goals set forth in his speech, any official advisory body specifically appointed for that task could not be expected to come in with the verdict that the president was simply wrong. Nevertheless, it is quite clear that those charged with executing the president's program do not share his optimism that nuclear weapons can be made "impotent and obsolete."[24] If the United States is to pursue a policy in the area of military technology along the lines advocated here, it will have to be led by at least one administration dedicated to that policy. But if it is to have continuity, such a policy would require the creation of a science advisory apparatus at least as independent and influential as was the PSAC.

The scientific community should not shrink from working toward the creation of a sound science advisory system. Scientists have an especially heavy responsibility in this area, because their creations are such an integral part of our predicament. As Solly Zuckerman, for many years the chief science adviser to the British Ministry of Defense and the British government has said,

> It is the man in the laboratory, not the soldier or sailor or airman, who at the start proposes that for this or that reason it would be useful to improve an old or devise a new nuclear warhead; and if a new warhead, then a new missile; and given a new missile, a new system within which it has to fit. It is he, the technician, not the commander in the field, who starts the process of formulating the so-called military need. . . . The men in the nuclear weapons laboratories of both sides have succeeded in creating a world with an irrational foundation, on which a new set of political realities has in turn to be built. They have become the alchemists of our times, working in secret ways that cannot be divulged, casting spells that embrace us all.[25]

That spell can only be broken by the scientific community itself, for only scientists can eradicate the misconception that the significance and implications of nuclear weapons can only be understood by "the experts." Nor should scientists shrink from advocating policies that mingle purely scientific matters with strategic and geopolitical factors, even if a secretary of state has asserted that they have no call on their fellow citizens' attention once they leave the domain of the purely technical.[26]

By and large, the scientific community has shown at least as much insight as anyone into the political implications of the awesome risks that science has created. As exhibit number one in support of this claim, consider the following excerpts from a report to the secretary of war, Henry Stimson, written by Arthur H. Compton, Enrico Fermi, Ernest O. Lawrence, and Robert J. Oppenheimer just eleven days after the bombing of Hiroshima:

> We have been unable to devise or propose effective military counter-measures for atomic weapons. Although we realize that future work may reveal possibilities at present obscure to us, it is our firm opinion that no military countermeasures will be found which will be adequately effective in preventing the delivery of atomic weapons. . . .

We are not only unable to outline a program that would ensure to the nation for the next decades hegemony in the field of atomic weapons; we are equally unable to insure that such hegemony, if achieved, could protect us from the most terrible destruction.

We believe that the safety of this nation—as opposed to its ability to inflict damage on an enemy power—cannot be wholly or even primarily in its scientific or technical prowess. It can only be based on making future wars impossible. It is our unanimous and urgent recommendation to you that, despite the present incomplete exploitation of technical possibilities in this field, all steps be taken, all necessary international arrangements be made to this one end.[27]

These words speak with greater force today than they did forty years ago, for they have been confirmed by history. The prophetic vision they embody is still the only guide to our survival.

NOTES

1. The text of this chapter is based on a lecture given by the author at the University of California, Santa Barbara, on 1 April 1985.
2. The development of the Soviet nuclear-weapons program is described in David Holloway, *The Soviet Union and the Arms Race,* second edition (New Haven, Conn.: Yale University Press, 1984), ch. 2.
3. *Los Angeles Times,* 4 April 1982.
4. See especially Desmond Ball, *International Security* 7, no. 3 (Winter 1982/1983); *Targeting for Strategic Deterrence,* Adelphi Paper no. 185 (London: International Institute for Strategic Studies [IISS], 1983).
5. Solly Zuckerman, *Nuclear Illusion and Reality* (New York: Viking, 1982), pp. 70 ff., provides a list of former chiefs of the British Defense Staff who hold such views. Senior U.S. military leaders, going back to Omar Bradley, Dwight Eisenhower, and Douglas MacArthur, have also expressed the belief that nuclear weapons could not serve military ends against an adversary that possessed them, and the current supreme allied commander in Europe, Gen. Bernard Rogers, has indicated that he holds grave reservations about NATO's reliance on nuclear weapons. Such considerations have led a number of former senior civilian officials and military officers to espouse a policy of "no first use"; see especially McGeorge Bundy, George F. Kennan, Robert S. McNamara, and Gerard C. Smith, *Foreign Affairs* 60, no. 4, 1982.
6. Bruce G. Blair, *Strategic Command and Control* (Washington, D.C.: Brookings Institution, 1985). Cleavages between nuclear doctrine and military reality are not unknown in the Soviet defense establishment; see Holloway, *The Soviet Union,* ch. 3.
7. Although silo defense is technically feasible, there is still the large question of whether it is desirable from a strategic and political point of view. We shall not enter into this point here; to my mind the strategic considerations that led the superpowers to the ABM Treaty are as valid in 1985 as they were when the treaty was signed in 1972.
8. This tactic is called "launch under attack." See Richard L. Garwin, *International Security* 4, no. 3 (Winter 1979/1980), pp. 117–139; and John Steinbruner, *Scientific American* 250, no. 1 (January 1984).

9. Aside from the Cuban missile crisis, there has been just one exception to this rule: the U.S. strategic alert triggered by the Yom Kippur War of 1973. See Scott Sagan, *International Security* 9, no. 4, 1985.

10. The political implications of this judgment are explored in Robert S. McNamara and Hans A. Bethe, *Atlantic*, July 1985.

11. The United States has a complete constellation of reliable early-warning satellites, whereas Soviet satellites that perform this mission appear to suffer from considerable technical problems and do not seem to provide full coverage of U.S. missile fields. See Nicholas L. Johnson, *The Soviet Year in Space: 1984* (Colorado Springs, Colo.: Teledyne Brown Engineering, 1985).

12. One might say that the early-warning satellites would also undergo this Jekyll-Hyde transition, because they would tell the attacked nation which missiles had been fired and could therefore be used to optimize retaliation. But that, at least, is a retort to aggression.

13. As an example of current interest, it would not really matter if one superpower thought it could formulate an interpretation of the ABM Treaty that would permit it to carry through a development program to the point where the other superpower believed that the first superpower was in a position to deploy a comprehensive missile defense. Well before that point was reached there would be a response, and not just in words, but in military hardware. In any event, arms control treaties provide each party with "the right to withdraw if it decides that extraordinary events . . . have jeopardized its supreme interests" (article XV of the ABM Treaty). It should be recognized, however, that it would be considerably more difficult for the United States to withdraw from a treaty under such circumstances, because the U.S. government would have to convince its electorate and its allies that such a drastic step was really necessary.

14. See, for example, "Verification," in *Challenges for U.S. National Security* (Washington, D.C.: Carnegie Endowment for International Peace, 1983); and Kosta Tsipis, David Hafemeister, and Penny Jamesway, eds., *Arms Control Verification: The Technology that Makes It Possible* (forthcoming).

15. See, for example, the proceedings of "The Nuclear Weapons Freeze and Arms Control," a symposium held at the American Academy of Arts and Sciences, Cambridge, Mass., 13–15 January 1983.

16. Soviet military forces, both nuclear and conventional, are described in *The Military Balance,* published annually by IISS, London. As an example of what is known about the Soviet military beyond its hardware, see Stephen M. Meyer, *Soviet Theater Nuclear Forces,* Adelphi Paper no. 187 (London: IISS, 1983/1984).

17. I owe this parable to Richard L. Garwin.

18. Richard L. Garwin, Kurt Gottfried, and Donald L. Hafner, *Scientific American* 250, no. 6 (June 1984); Kurt Gottfried and Richard Ned Lebow, *Daedalus,* Summer 1985.

19. For statements concerning this by several serving and retired government experts on space surveillance, see R. Jeffrey Smith, *Science,* 18 May 1984, pp. 693–696.

20. *Strategic Missile Defense: Necessities, Prospects, and Dangers in the Near Term,* A Special Report of the Center for International Security and Arms Control (Stanford Calif.: Board of Trustees of Leland Stanford Junior University, 1985).

21. See n. 14.

22. See n. 5.

23. See Richard L. Garwin, "Presidential Science Advising," *Technology in Society* 2, nos. 1 and 2 (1980), pp. 115–128.

24. For the views of the chief scientist of the Strategic Defense Initiative Organization, see G. Yonas, *Physics Today,* June 1985, pp. 24–32.

25. See Zuckerman, *Nuclear Illusion,* pp. 105–106.

26. See *Science,* 22 March 1985, p. 1446.

27. Alice Kimball Smith and Charles Weiner, eds., *Robert Oppenheimer: Letters and Recollections* (Cambridge: Harvard University Press, 1980), pp. 293–294.

8

TRANSFORMING INTERNATIONAL SECURITY CONFLICTS

ERNST-OTTO CZEMPIEL

Global peace and security are goals shared by all humanity. Although there have been, and still are, exceptions, it can be assumed that no modern industrialized state is interested in warfare. Prosperity depends on peace, and nuclear weapons have made security, not military victory, the supreme goal. Nonetheless, the countries of the North Atlantic Treaty Organization (NATO) and the Warsaw Pact confront each other within the system of mutual deterrence. They have built up their armaments to such a degree that there are ample overkill capabilities. East and West can destroy each other several times over, and yet both sides are engaged in research and development to create more sophisticated weapons. During the early 1980s there has been a new Cold War between East and West, with relations strained and contacts weakened, with arms control almost dead. How could this happen? If the interests of all states in the East-West conflict point toward peace, not war, why then all these armaments? Why do we have in the East-West conflict a situation in which war is to be avoided but, in principle, not excluded? What is the explanation for a situation in which everybody speaks in favor of peace and security and yet behaves in a way that seems to favor war preparation and arms buildup?

The reason for this contradiction is not difficult to find. People and politicians have grown accustomed to the contradictions of the system of deterrence. The so-called Harmel formula of NATO (1967), which offers to the Soviet Union defense and cooperation, combines the possibility of peace for all with the reality of security for the

West. This combination has worked effectively for almost twenty years and has produced that fragile but stable relationship that we are used to calling the East-West conflict. But that conflict is basically contradictory. Cooperation and preparation for war are not complementary, and the arms race has won out. The contradiction between the goal of peace and security and the means of war preparation and deterrence can be explained by custom. We live and think within this contradictory system of deterrence, and we have stopped reflecting on it. We argue immanently, without permanent reconsideration of the whole East-West conflict. We do not look at it from the outside, we act from within. Custom has replaced consideration.

CONTRADICTIONS WITHIN
THE EAST-WEST CONFLICT

For the political scientist, however, the contradictions within the East-West conflict remain contradictions. They reveal that what is going on between East and West is a real international conflict of tremendous size but traditional substance. There have been arms races throughout modern history, and we know a lot about them and their rationales.[1] They have been part and parcel of larger conflicts, stemming from competition for territory, people, and resources.[2] There have been conflicts about power.[3] If armaments and arms races indicate the existence of an international conflict, what is the East-West conflict about? What is its substance? Are East and West competing for territories, people, resources? Is power the object of our conflict with Moscow? Nobody would answer these questions in the affirmative. Nobody would point to Moscow as a potential military aggressor or select the military threat as the heart of the political matter. Seen from outside, from the vantage point of political science, the East-West conflict has always been a political conflict, which has figured as a predominantly, if not exclusively, military confrontation only for the last twenty-five years. In reality, the East-West conflict covers a broad range of areas of competition—political, ideological, economic—which are veiled behind the military competition.

This broad range of conflict makes plausible the apparent contradictions within the system of mutual deterrence. By itself, it could not be explained except by the security dilemma[4] that stems from the anarchical structure of the international system. We have to pull out from the dark the forgotten issues of diverging societal concepts, of competing ideologies, and of the struggle for power and influence in the Third World. In other words, global peace and security will be served only if we reconstitute our understanding of the relations between East and West as a real international conflict, touching many issue areas and containing several outcomes.

The benefit of doing so will be twofold. First, global peace can be attained only if we succeed in demilitarizing the East-West conflict. There will be peace on earth only if this "deadly quarrel"[5] loses its vigor, perhaps ceases to exist. Second, our security will be enhanced tremendously if, in striving for peace, we can manage to shift the emphasis of the East-West conflict from the military to the political and social fields. This must be done anyway, because the conflict extends to these areas as well. But the immediate benefit of shifting the focus to other issue areas would be to diminish the saliency of the military one and so somewhat weaken the arms race. Mutual deterrence will remain in place, but it might be possible to put a cap on the arms race and to the same degree enhance security. Only by such a strategy can we combine defense with cooperation, can we realize the Harmel formula.

This is the strategy of conflict transformation. During the search for a solution to the conflict, its different components could be emphasized differently. Sometimes the competition for political power and influence could be stressed, sometimes the ideological struggle. Military power is inevitable but should be kept in reserve only.

Conflict can be treated in several and different ways: This is the general lesson. Conflicts have many dimensions interacting with each other and producing intertwined complexities. To understand these complexities and to use them for the transformation of conflicts from the issue of security to less dangerous issue areas—this is the general political task. This paper, therefore, selects as its primary topic the transformation of international conflicts—a transformation that comes as close as possible to the goal we all cherish: peace.

THE CONNECTIONS BETWEEN PEACE AND SECURITY

In order to analyze peace and security from this point of view, some more general observations are necessary. Peace, security, and conflict are terms of the conventional language. But they are imprecise. Not even political science has developed a precise and generally accepted understanding of what the term "international conflict" really means.[6] In the East-West conflict, for example, who is in conflict with whom?—governments, states, alliances, societies, economies, ideologies? politicians, diplomats, soldiers? What are these conflicting about?—power, profit, influence, security, or victory? On the macro-level of politics (and this is the level of conventional wisdom), everything seems to be simple and obvious. On the micro-level of politics (and this is the level where policies are developed and executed), nobody knows exactly what is being done by whom, for whom, and why. Most analyses of the East-West conflict remain, therefore, on the macro-level of description.

Analysts speak of the conflict between the Soviet Union and the United States, East and West, as if everyone knew the processes and the contents.[7] Certainly, there has been Joseph Stalin, the Soviet rule in Eastern Europe, the 1968 invasion of Czechoslovakia, and the 1979 invasion of Afghanistan. Certainly, there is a repressive system in the Soviet Union, the totalitarian ideology of orthodox communism. Nobody denies this. But this is only part of the story, and many parts of it are already history. On the other hand, the competition between liberalism and communism has become worldwide, with many countries of the Third World leaning toward neutrality. There is the competition between two models of economies and societies, one with the market, the other with the state, at its center. There is the struggle between two ideologies, one serving the individual, the other the society. And there is the arms race, and also economic exchange and competition.

On the micro-level, what are the contents of the East-West conflict? What does the term conflict really mean, and which goals are mutually exclusive, incompatible, different, nonidentical? The content of these four terms is not at all the same. Ends that are incompatible are not necessarily mutually exclusive. If we determine—as the wisdom of political science would have it[8]—that conflict exists if ends are incompatible, what consequences follow for our understanding of conflict resolution? To make compatible what has been by definition incompatible is possible only by sheer force. This is what the historical record seems to indicate. If we exclude force as an acceptable kind of conflict resolution—because we are not inclined to suffer it and not willing to impose it on our adversaries—what kind of resolution can we conceive of?

To answer this question, we need a more detailed understanding of conflict. As a clash of incompatible goals or interests, it is a fact of daily life. Whenever we do something, we meet other people not doing the same thing, having different, eventually incompatible interests. Only in rare cases are these conflicts resolved by the use of force. Mostly, people try to win by persuasion. Sometimes, they are ready to compromise, or they simply agree not to agree. The various ways to treat a conflict between incompatible goals can be rank-ordered on a continuum, ranging from the extreme of killing the opponent to the other pole of the continuum, the compromise. In each of these cases the conflict is resolved. In all other cases it is treated but remains intact. Such treatment differs according to the degree of violence involved; at this point the notion of peace becomes relevant. If conflicts are a fact of international life, then peace means not the absence of conflict, but rather its nonviolent treatment. There may but need not be a compromise; other ways of handling incompatible interests range from toleration to nonviolent competition and struggle. In domestic politics in democratic countries this order has already been accepted. Parties, politicians, and interest groups fight each other with tangible consequences for the distribution of values; they do not use force, and if they do they are prosecuted.

In the international system the role of the judge is, in a way, played by the interest in peace. Global peace then means to treat all conflict in a nonviolent manner, to reduce the degree of force, and to develop nonviolent forms of handling incompatible interests. Of course, this is easier said than done.

A relationship probably exists between the content of a conflict and the means of its treatment. If the conflict is over territory and people (as is often the case in preindustrial societies) military force might be the only available solution. Conflicts of this kind arise within the Third World and are certain to continue to do so in the future. If the issue is economic profit, force is mostly dysfunctional. If political and social systems are incompatible, propaganda or the setting of good examples might be pertinent; force certainly would not be. But the relationship between the content of a conflict and the means of treating it is not a deterministic one—with perhaps one exception. If a country is attacked, defense is necessary. This is true, however, only when the attack comes suddenly, unanticipated, and without any chance of being contained. Otherwise, choices may be made in the handling of every conflict.

The concept of transforming international conflicts rests on the fact that such choice is possible, that there is no fixed relationship between the contents of a conflict and the means of its treatment. One conflict may be treated in different ways; it may even be possible (although admittedly difficult) to avert an imminent aggression. Putting aside this extreme case, the essence of transforming international conflicts means not to solve them, not to neglect them, not to underestimate them, but to face them—and to change their outlook.

THE TRANSFORMATION OF CONFLICTS

Conflict transformation offers a political possibility that did not exist before the nineteenth century, when democracy and capitalism entered the historical scene. In former times, when kings and knights fought each other, the issues were clear and the options limited. In today's East-West conflict, complex societies confront each other over several and diffuse issues that are related to the domestic texture of those societies. It is not easy to "move a nation," as Roger Hilsman showed in his analysis:[9] Modern developed societies are inward oriented; they look for internal progress rather than for external processes.

Because modern conflicts have many facets, the relationship between the conflicts and the societies involved changes over time and is open to influence. It has become difficult to define how the conflict and its elements are spread among the various actors and segments of populations. Attitudes change from actor to actor and may even contradict each other. For example, the business community has different interests and perceptions than do the general public or the politicians. The U.S. Chamber of Commerce has consistently voted in favor of continuing détente with the Soviet Union, although the administration has turned to a more confrontational course. In the Soviet Union the new generation of political leaders may treat the conflict with the West differently than the older generation did, and with a different set of political priorities.

Because developed societies have become so complex and international conflicts have become intertwined with domestic structure and decision making, conflicts have lost their one-dimensional quality. Accordingly, more options offer themselves to politicians, who can choose whether to stress the economic or the political issue, the ideological or the military one, whether to favor a confrontational policy or to offer cooperation. Obviously, such choices are not perfectly free. They depend also on the behavior of the opponent, but not entirely. Theoretically, when the power of states is in balance, then freedom of action is distributed more or less equally, and each state enjoys the same measure of freedom to act and necessity to react. Of course, the actual distribution depends on the concrete historical case. The point here is that the status of a conflict depends on the behavior of its participants; they have the capacity to steer the conflict in the direction they choose.

Thus, the tactics of conflict transformation involve the exploitation of the complexity of modern international conflicts, making use of their linkage to various parts of the populations, in order to influence the way conflict is developing. The contemporary politician enjoys a capability denied his predecessors, namely, to direct the course of history. What used to be fate has become challenge. Nuclear weapons produced as a necessity what would otherwise have only been an opportunity: the avoidance of war and the nonviolent treatment of international conflicts. Albert Einstein was correct in assuming that nuclear weapons would demand the development of a new political conscience,[10] but, from the viewpoint of political science, that new conscience depends not only on modern weapons of mass destruction but, in particular, on the modern situation of industrialized democracies. This development demands (and makes possible) a new handling of international conflicts.

Transforming international conflicts does not mean solving them. As mentioned earlier, conflict can be ended only by killing—or being killed by—the adversary, or by finding a compromise. It is open to question whether a compromise really solves the conflict or produces only a temporary stalemate. It is possible that international conflicts become outdated, as certainly was the case with the religious wars in Europe. The conflict between France and Germany, which dominated the second half of the nineteenth and the first half of the twentieth century, has come to an end. But two devastating wars were needed to produce this result, although there certainly had been two chances, in 1890 and in the late 1920s, to transform this conflict into stages of lesser and, eventually, no violence. But they were missed.

International conflicts need not end. It is possible to live with them, to tolerate them, even to foster them—assuming always that violence is avoided. Above, I compared this possibility with the domestic situation of a state. Of course, one cannot compare the international system with a national one. But with regard to violence the similarity has grown. The concept of peacekeeping developed by the United Nations under Dag Hammarskjöld concentrated upon the avoidance of warfare and sought to separate the solution of the conflict from the way of treating it, similar to what happens in a functioning domestic system. Peacekeeping was meant to keep the adversaries from fighting each other and to urge them to find other means of handling the conflict. For example, even if the questions of the West Bank, the Golan Heights, the Gaza strip, and the Palestinian homeland were to be solved, there would still remain the conflict between Israel and its Arab neighbors. This conflict could be tolerated, perhaps even for decades, so long as no arms were used. If it is impossible to find solutions for international conflicts, it is certainly possible to move from violence toward nonmilitary means in their treatment.

Indeed, to reduce the complex structure of conflict to the military field might miss its substance altogether. This is what the Soviets experienced in Afghanistan. No differences with regard to territory, resources, and power justified the military invasion. Rather, the conflict stemmed from religious and ideological differences. Most certainly, the Soviet Union could have afforded to live with those differences, to tolerate a somewhat deviant government in Kabul. Moscow could have tried to influence the situation in Afghanistan by offering ideological and material help and by exerting political influence.

The small chance that these means would have succeeded was forgone when Moscow resorted to military invasion, which, by necessity, missed the goal because it missed the point. The preference for military force is a remnant of the middle ages, when most, if not all, conflicts were based on territorial claims that could be settled by occupation only. In modern times the structure of international conflicts is much more complicated. The substance of a "modern" conflict is less over territory but activates so many different layers of interests that war has lost its meaning and will not settle anything. Perhaps it is this insight that has, within the East-West conflict, contributed as much as the existence of nuclear weapons to keeping the peace and avoiding the conflagration.

VARIOUS LEVELS OF THE EAST-WEST CONFLICT

Everything I have said so far is borne out by East and West in their contemporary conflict, the focus of which rests with the military confrontation exclusively. The other components are neglected; in fact, in concentrating upon the arms race both sides have lost sight of the elements that really underlie their conflict. Reducing it to a mere military confrontation might be easy and convenient because such a confrontation can be made convincingly and demonstratively, but it puts the cart before the horse. The East-West conflict never has been a military one; it contains no elements that could be resolved by destruction. It possesses, on the other hand, many vigorous differences in areas such as legitimacy, prosperity, political participation, and justice, which cannot be addressed by guns and missiles. A shift in emphasis back to these issues would revitalize the real divisions between East and West and thus transform this conflict.

The East-West conflict started in 1917 with the Bolshevik revolution. The Western powers tried in vain to extinguish the revolution, then slowly accepted the Soviet Union as a new junior partner in the international system.[11] During World War II the Western powers and the Soviet Union cooperated against Germany and its allies; after 1945, they tried to conserve this cooperation. It is open to question in what year the Cold War really began.[12] Of interest here is the fact that the conflict between communism in its Bolshevik version and the liberalism of the West experienced many different stages, ranging from military invasion to cooperation. The conflict remained the same, with the antagonistic competition between two societal systems at its core.

The East-West conflict underwent many phases after 1945 as well.[13] From 1945 to 1947 there was cooperation with suspicion. In 1947 the Cold War began and continued until the first Geneva summit (1955) inaugurated the first stage of détente. After the Cuban missile crisis in 1962, the second phase of détente began; from 1969 on, détente was furthered by the policies of the Nixon administration. Because of Soviet rearmament, starting in 1963, détente came to a partial end around the mid-1970s, when the United States found itself forced to rearm in order to keep pace with the Soviet Union. After 1980 the situation deteriorated to what was commonly called the second wave of the Cold War, which seemed to ebb to a certain degree after 1984. The details of this development after 1945 do not matter here. The point is the see-saw performance the East-West conflict has produced since 1917 and, above all, since 1945. This underlines the thesis that an international conflict is not fixed in its nature once and forever but is a flexible formation of divergent positions that can accept, tolerate, or even demand different behavior.

Not only do conflicts change their outlook; they also alter their composition. At its center the East-West conflict consists of the antagonistic differences between two versions of political legitimacy, two societal orders. The way to handle this central conflict is competition between the two systems, with no "victory" in its traditional sense as its outcome. The winner is the societal order that best fulfills the aspirations of the people, answering their demands and converting them into outputs that are effective and just. But after 1945, the East-West conflict assembled a number of other layers around this center. The first stemmed from the security dilemma arising out of the decay of wartime cooperation. After cooperation broke down, over the partition of Germany and other issues, suspicion arose. Both sides started to build military alliances as a safety measure.

In 1950 another layer was added. North Korea invaded South Korea, and the West became convinced that the Soviet Union was trying to expand its influence into the Third World, at that time predominantly Western-oriented (as it perhaps had already done in 1947 in Greece and Turkey). Whether this interpretation was correct or not, since then the East-West conflict has become a competition for influence in the Third World. Alliances were augmented, armaments enhanced; the policy of containment obtained a global meaning.

After extending over the globe, the East-West conflict then became military in nature, marked by the explosion of the first Soviet hydrogen bomb in 1954 and, above all, by the Soviet Sputnik in 1957. The conflict developed a layer of military threat and counterthreat. But this was a thin layer. With the exception of central Europe, where after 1948 the East-West conflict had a strong military outlook, the military aspect had only been peripheral to the competition. The Third World was more or less still under colonial rule, and its political relevance was rather small. All this changed rapidly in the 1960s, when colonialism was ended and the Soviet Union started its huge rearmament with the intention of becoming the second military superpower. After the West realized Soviet intentions and accepted this challenge, a fourth layer was added to the East-West conflict: the arms race. With the Soviet Union pushing ahead and the United States trying successfully to catch up, the arms race in the 1970s and in the 1980s became the centerpiece of the East-West conflict. Arms races tend to forget their origins. They fuel themselves on competition.

In 1985 we have a remarkable situation in the East-West conflict: Attention is focused almost exclusively on the Soviet military threat and the response of the West—in other words, on the arms race. Competition over influence in the Third World has also taken on a predominantly military outlook: The Soviet Union has taken the lead by appearing in the Horn of Africa and on the shores of Vietnam, with the West following suit. All the other problems posed by the Third World—economic, social, and political—are more or less neglected, as is the original center of the East-West conflict. No one speaks anymore about the competition between communism and liberalism, legitimacies and political systems, liberties and rights. They are mentioned, but only as a tool to castigate the other side. They are not accepted as the central issue area, in which the heart of the conflict really lies and in which the fate of the conflict will be decided.

As history bears out, conflicts change their outlook and their composition. They are in constant flux. They attract new layers of competition and shift the focus of attention from layer to layer. What is of interest here is this process of constant transformation of the conflict. It has been experienced within the East-West conflict but has not, except in the détente process of the 1970s, been used explicitly by the West as a political instrument. The transformation of the East-West conflict has happened but was not consciously made. The task before us, therefore, is to profit from theory and to learn from history in order to develop a strategy of conflict transformation. In the case of the East-West conflict this means to rediscover the central elements of the competition and to shift the focus there. A shift in focus would enhance peace (understood as the nonviolent treatment of conflicts) and would benefit security because the military confrontation could be softened, although it would not disappear. The security dilemma will remain, and the competition for influence in the Third World probably demands some military posture, but perhaps smaller than what both sides are preparing today. The military posture could give way to competition for the political and economic orientation of Third World countries. A strategy of transforming the East-West conflict that returns it to its original elements would serve at the same time the goal of global peace and security.

A STRATEGY FOR PEACE AND SECURITY

The task of developing such a strategy is facilitated considerably by reflecting on what former generations of politicians and theorists have already found. Of course, they did not use the term "conflict transformation" and did not live under conditions in which such a transformation could be consciously tried. Their term of reference was "peace," a goal unattainable in those times, and perhaps in ours as well. But they addressed the same problem facing us today: how to avoid violence in international conflicts. Historical circumstances and political conditions have changed, but the problem has remained the same.

The history of thinking on war and peace suggests that the best method for conflict transformation is offered by the establishment of an international organization. The concept dates back to the writings of Pierre Dubois (1306) and the Bohemian King George of Podebrad (1464); it was reconsidered and enlarged by the Abbé de Saint-Pierre (1713–1716) and by Immanuel Kant (1796); it was adapted and modernized by the U.S.-European peace movement in the nineteenth century; and, finally, it was realized in the League of Nations after World War I and, after World War II, in the United Nations.[14] Reviewing this history of almost 1,200 years brings to mind three observations. First, no alternatives have been found for conflict transformation other than international organization, which offers the best instrument by directly influencing international interaction. Second, the functions and effectiveness of international organization have been interpreted differently over the centuries. And third, whenever actual international organizations were put to a test, the idea was abandoned.

Perhaps the first observation is the most important one. The literature about the preservation of peace and security (which, by the way, is not numerous) reveals, surprisingly, that all international theories point to the international organization. Of course, most politicians have shied away from this idea; they have relied upon the force of arms and have produced the traditional results—war. The only alternative concept that was developed was that of international organization. The fact that the concept has not functioned as desired should not detract from its salience. Its success depends on the foreign policies of the conflict parties going along. International organization is an instrument of international policies; it cannot replace but can give incentives and opportunities to foreign policy. The international organization is the only tool that can change the character of the international system. In this capacity, it is outstanding. All the more disappointing is its failure up to now.

There are several explanations for this. The most interesting one is that the organization established in 1945 did not follow the concepts of the eighteenth and nineteenth centuries. The United Nations was founded as an instrument of collective security, as was also the case with the League of Nations. They tried to organize and to institutionalize the mechanism of the balance of power practiced by the concert of nations in the world of the nineteenth century. This differed considerably from the international organization in its original conception, whose basic idea was not collective security—although this was included—but rather the notion that a commonwealth of nations would acknowledge the members' right to exist and agree therefore to the nonviolent handling of international conflicts. A utopian idea under the conditions of those times, it pointed in the right direction. An international organization comes into being only if there is a common purpose. At the same time, this common purpose is fostered and enhanced by the international organization.

The effect may be weak, but it is real because the context of the international system has changed. Anarchy and insecurity are replaced by organization and information, the security dilemma diminishes accordingly, and the stimulus to handle international conflicts nonviolently grows. Interaction augments interdependence, which in time changes the outlook of international conflicts. What in the traditional international system appeared to be a traditional conflict with military means takes on a completely different shape within the context of international organization. The substance of the conflict remains unchanged, but a different method is used for its treatment. The situation is not similar to, but is nonetheless analogous to, the domestic scene. The international organization remains part of the international system, and therefore military violence is not excluded forever but remains an available course of action. But it becomes the method of last resort, ranking far behind other ways of handling a conflict.

What the daily interaction of nations within the international organization produces is a shift of emphasis from violent to nonviolent means.

With its orientation toward collective security, the United Nations had great difficulties surviving when cooperation between the great powers broke down because of the Cold War. Both sides, in effect, left the international organization. The East-West conflict was not handled within, but outside of, the United Nations. Both sides neglected the immense progress that had been made with the foundation of the United Nations and took refuge in the old traditional concept of military alliances. Perhaps these alliances were unavoidable, given the mutual distrust after 1946 and the resulting security dilemma. But it is appalling that the East-West conflict was, with only a few exceptions, kept totally out of the international organization and was entrusted exclusively to military methods. Both sides quickly forgot the possibilities offered by an international organization and abandoned the instrument altogether. Since then the United Nations has not been used in any comprehensive way for the purpose of negotiating the East-West conflict but has been used primarily for handling conflict between smaller nations; in this capacity, the UN has developed and practiced the pertinent concept of peacekeeping.

For their own conflict, the powers preferred the traditional machinery of war preparation and deterrence. They followed Vegetius, who in the fifth century formulated the concept that theorists of international organization have convincingly demonstrated to be dysfunctional: *Si vis pacem, para bellum* (If you wish peace, prepare for war).[15] Deterrence works for a while, but it does not produce either peace or security. Did the West try to influence the Soviet Union, to lure it away from violent and repressive behavior? Was the United Nations used for documenting and stressing the goals common to both the West and the East, notably the avoidance of war? Was it necessary to keep the treatment of the East-West conflict totally out of the United Nations? If all these questions have to be answered in the affirmative because the Soviet Union under Stalin was a totalitarian monolith and could not be influenced by any means other than military pressure, why is it that the international organization is not used today for handling the conflict between East and West? Many secretaries-general of the UN have argued that governments "have strayed far from the Charta . . . [and] believe they can win an international objective by force"[16] and have stressed the importance of the UN "as an alternative to the kind of confrontation which, in our nuclear age, could well be fatal to us all."[17] Secretary-General U Thant was certainly right when, in his farewell address to the United

Nations, he argued that "nations and people will turn their backs on this great endeavour at their gravest peril."[18]

To give up on international organizations amounts to turning the clock of the international system back to the seventeenth century, when Thomas Hobbes correctly analyzed it as a "war of all against all." On the other hand, using international organizations as the appropriate forums for handling international conflicts would help change the international system and recognize existing interdependencies—not the least of which is the common interest to avoid a nuclear holocaust. The mere fact that contending nations meet each other within an international organization changes the context of their conflict. Indeed, interaction within an international organization would be one of the most important contributions to the transformation of international security conflicts. It would diminish the security dilemma by making the actors better known to each other and by making their behavior more transparent. This would help slow down the arms race, which is partly fueled by uncertainty about the behavior of the opponent. Here lies the problem of the arms control talks of our time: They are an isolated endeavor to cooperate within a sea of mistrust and noninteraction. The context creates misperceptions and predetermines failure. It is impossible to put into the context of general conflict the most sensitive and contentious East-West problem.

If put in the context of an international organization, this contradiction would evaporate. Arms control would be embedded in a wider array of interactions, which would contribute to the impression that all parties mean business. Of course, arms control negotiations would remain most delicate and difficult. All sides must be prepared to make concessions. But the international organization would provide a setting that gives credibility to the endeavor. It would be easier to test the sincerity of all parties because their cooperation within the organization would demonstrate it.

In the international system there will always be the outsider, the deviator, the potential aggressor. This was the role played by the Soviet Union in the late 1940s and 1950s. The Soviet posture was the primary reason for the Western powers' reliance on military alliance rather than on the international organization—understandable, but perhaps wrong. The international organization itself enlarges the context for cooperation; thus the West abandoned the only instrument capable of influencing the USSR. This contextual effect of international organization was already known to the statesmen of the nineteenth century. Metternich and Castlereagh knew very well that conferences and congresses, the prestages of an international organization, were able to influence the enemy, to "group-in" the deviator.[19]

More than a century later UN Secretary-General U Thant described this function of the international organization as exposing all member states "to the impact of the work of the organization and to the currents and cross-currents of opinion that prevail within it."[20] This insight should have helped to manage the conflict with the Soviet Union. There is no better way to influence the deviator than to group the deviator in. This insight could also help to reintegrate the East-West conflict into the United Nations. There it would look completely different than it does on the outside. Within the organization there would be a strong and unabated struggle between East and West for the best societal order and for power and influence in the world. Military confrontation and war would remain a possibility, but a more remote one. Outside the international organization the possibility of war is enlarged considerably. Most likely the arms race would never have dominated the East-West conflict had the conflict been kept within the United Nations framework.

International organization does not mean only the United Nations; its principles work whenever cooperation is institutionalized. This can happen in permanent conferences or regularly convened congresses. The Helsinki process, for example, is such an undertaking, and it is worthwhile to keep it alive. Whatever concessions the Soviet Union has made, they would not have been possible without this semipermanent conference. The same is true for the Conference on Confidence- and Security-Building Measures and Disarmament in Europe (CDE). Its deliberations have proven difficult, but they have the prospect of success.

DEMILITARIZING THE EAST-WEST CONFLICT

International organizations contain the best available strategy for transforming international security conflicts. They facilitate the avoidance of a military, nuclear conflict. Nobody wants such a conflict, because it would be the end of our world; but given the dynamics of the security dilemma and the arms race, nations follow the path of producing more and more dangerous arms. International organizations could help to stop the vicious mechanism and could facilitate putting the focus of the conflict back to where it belongs. To make use of the transforming capabilities of the international organization would have an additional short-term advantage for the West. The Soviet Union has managed to expand its influence in the Third World considerably; the West, by concentrating on military instruments, has lost ground in the Third World. For the Third World the conflict between East and West is of secondary importance to economic development. Former presidential adviser Zbigniew Brzezinski was correct in asking for a "constructive global engagement" of the United States in favor of human rights all over the world.[21] Former Secretary of State Cyrus Vance was even more correct in suggesting that Third World problems be treated in their own right and not as an appendix of the East-West military competition.[22] The political and societal conflict with the Soviet Union will be won by the West only if it succeeds in convincing the Third World that liberalism and the market economy fulfill the expectations of the people better than communism does. This is the real conflict.

Transforming the East-West conflict from its military to its political layer would benefit the West immediately, because in the political and economic fields the West has a clear and undisputed superiority over communism. Western democracy, not "people's democracy," fulfills the aspirations of the people. Military power is the only field in which the Soviet Union can successfully compete with the West. Demilitarizing the conflict, shifting its emphasis back to politics and economics, would stress the Western advantages immediately and immensely. The Western countries can only lose if they permit themselves to continue to be dragged into the arms race.

But more important than these tactical considerations, the East-West conflict must be transformed into its original political configuration because only then are global peace and security promoted. Security cannot be guaranteed by mutual deterrence, along with some elements of arms control, because the arms race threatens to get out of control. Global security can be enhanced only if the military confrontation is diminished and gives way to the political competition. This political conflict will probably go on for decades to come, because no solution (except by mutual annihilation) can be imagined. But, as we have seen, it is not necessary to solve the conflict. It is enough to treat it without military violence. Political conflicts exist even in the domestic policies of nations; they will certainly go on indefinitely within the international system. Only when this conflict reaches a stage in which the use of arms is definitely excluded will global peace be attained. Because the international organization can contribute to such a transformation of conflict, it should be rediscovered and put to use.

NOTES

1. Lewis F. Richardson, *Arms and Insecurity* (Pittsburgh: Boxwood Press, 1960).

2. For a persuasive interpretation of these developments, see Wolfram F. Hanrieder, "Dissolving International Politics: Reflections on the Nation-State," *American Political Science Review* 72 (December 1978):127 ff.

3. This is stressed by the "realist school." See James E. Dougherty and Robert L. Pfaltzgraff, Jr., *Contending Theories of International Relations* (New York: Harper & Row, 1981), pp. 84 ff.

4. John H. Herz, *Political Realism and Political Idealism* (Chicago: University of Chicago Press, 1951).

5. This is the title of another book by Lewis F. Richardson, *Statistics of Deadly Quarrels* (Pittsburgh: Boxwood Press, 1960).

6. See Dougherty and Pfaltzgraff, *Contending Theories of International Relations,* pp. 181 ff., 251 ff.

7. See, for example, Lloyd C. Gardner, *A Covenant with Power: America and World Order from Wilson to Reagan* (New York: Oxford University Press, 1984).

8. See, for example, Kurt Singer, "The Meaning of Conflict," *Australian Journal of Philosophy* 27 (1949):145 ff.

9. Roger Hilsman, *To Move a Nation: The Politics of Foreign Policy of the Administration of John F. Kennedy* (New York: Doubleday, 1967).

10. Albert Einstein: "The unleashed power of the atom has changed everything except our thinking. Thus, we are drifting toward catastrophe beyond conception. We shall require a substantially new manner of thinking if mankind is to survive."

11. See George F. Kennan, *Soviet-American Relations, 1917–1920* (Princeton, N.J.: Princeton University Press, 1956).

12. Lynn E. Davis, *The Cold War Begins* (Princeton, N.J.: Princeton University Press, 1974).

13. Kjell Goldmann, *Tension and Détente in Bipolar Europe* (Stockholm, 1974).

14. See Abbott A. Brayton and Stephana J. Landwehr, *The Politics of War and Peace: A Survey of Thought* (Washington, D.C.: University Press of America, 1981).

15. See Michael Wallace, "Old Nails in New Coffins: The Para-Bellum Hypothesis Revisited," *Journal of Peace Research* 18, no. 1 (1981):91 ff.

16. United Nations, General Assembly, *Report of the Secretary-General on the Work of the Organization,* GAOR: Supplement no. 1 (A/37/1), 37th Session, p. 1.

17. Ibid., Supplement no. 1 (A/34/1), 34th Session, p. 1.

18. Ibid., Supplement no. IA (A/8401/add. 1), 26th Session, p. 17.

19. Richard B. Elrod, "The Concept of Europe: A Fresh Look at an International System," *World Politics* 28, no. 2 (January 1976):168.

20. United Nations, General Assembly, *Introduction to the Annual Report of the Secretary-General on the Work of the Organization,* GAOR (A/6301/add. 1), p. 14.

21. Zbigniew Brzezinski, *Power and Principle: Memoirs of the National Security Adviser 1977–1981* (New York: Farrar, Straus, Giroux, 1983).

22. Cyrus Vance, *Hard Choices: Critical Years in America's Foreign Policy* (New York: Simon and Schuster, 1983).

9

A CHRISTIAN RESPONSE
TO THE ARMS RACE

BISHOP THOMAS J. GUMBLETON

On 3 May 1983, the National Conference of Catholic Bishops entered the public policy debate on nuclear arms in a very clear way.[1] Their pastoral letter directly challenged the current public policy of the United States in a number of areas. The most dramatic challenge was the moral judgment of the bishops on the strategy of deterrence. In very careful words the bishops indicated that "considerations of concrete elements of nuclear deterrence policy . . . lead us to a strictly conditioned moral acceptance of nuclear deterrence. We cannot consider it adequate as a long-term basis for peace."[2] The bishops went on to say that "this strictly conditioned judgment yields criteria for morally assessing the elements of deterrence strategy. . . . These criteria require continual public scrutiny of what our government proposes to do with the deterrent."[3]

The criteria that must be used to make the continued moral assessment called for by the bishops are basically two:

1. Nuclear deterrence may exist only to prevent the use of nuclear weapons by others; hence, "sufficiently" to deter is an adequate strategy. Any proposals to go beyond this, e.g., the quest for nuclear superiority or planning for prolonged periods of repeated nuclear strikes and counterstrikes, or "prevailing" in nuclear war, are not acceptable.
2. Nuclear deterrence must be used as a step on the way toward progressive disarmament.[4]

This very carefully delineated judgment was arrived at by the bishops only after a very prolonged and difficult debate, first within the committee preparing the text of the pastoral and then among the whole body of bishops. It is a judgment that definitely does not satisfy many others who have tried to make a moral assessment of the strategy of deterrence. Many would want a clear-cut judgment that deterrence is certainly and unconditionally a moral way of acting. In fact, many of these would even assert that the United States has a moral obligation to follow a strategy of deterrence. On the other side, of course, are those who call for an outright condemnation of the strategy of deterrence.

> Indeed, we do acknowledge that there are many strong voices within our own episcopal ranks and within the wider Catholic community in the United States which challenge the strategy of deterrence as an adequate response to the arms race today. . . . Moreover, these voices rightly raise the concern that even the conditional acceptance of nuclear deterrence as laid out in a letter such as this might be inappropriately used by some to reinforce the policy of arms buildup.[5]

To understand why there is such a range of opinion about the moral assessment of deterrence, and why the bishops finally set forth a judgment that deterrence is morally acceptable only within strict conditions, it is important to acknowledge the very real dilemma presented by this strategy. First of all, everyone will acknowledge that the strategy of deterrence has a very important and good purpose— to prevent the use of nuclear weapons. "The moral duty today is to prevent nuclear war from ever occurring *and* to protect and preserve those key values of justice, freedom and independence which are necessary for personal dignity and national integrity."[6]

And many people will tell you that the policy of deterrence has worked now for almost four decades. No nuclear device has been exploded over any city since 9 August 1945. Perhaps it is because of deterrence. No one knows for sure, of course, why these weapons have not been used. But if it is because of the arsenals on each side, then it could be morally irresponsible simply to dismantle the weapons unilaterally. Perhaps we would evoke aggression, cause smaller nations to be attacked and taken over, perhaps even be drawn into a war ourselves. We would have failed to carry out the most important moral duty we have, "to prevent nuclear war from ever occurring."

But even though we grant that the purpose of deterrence is of extreme importance, we must also acknowledge that it is a strategy with the most serious moral defects. It is morally flawed in an inescapable way. There are a number of reasons why this is the case. The first is the unacceptable risk the deterrent imposes on all of creation. It is a continuing threat to human survival—and the survival of other species. As we declared in the pastoral letter:

> At the center of the Church's teaching on peace and at the center of all Catholic social teaching are the transcendence of God and the dignity of the human person. The human person is the clearest reflection of God's presence in the world; all of the Church's work in pursuit of both justice and peace is designed to protect and promote the dignity of every person. For each person not only reflects God, but is the expression of God's creative work and the meaning of Christ's redemptive ministry. Christians approach the problem of war and peace with fear and reverence. God is the lord of life, and so each human life is sacred; modern warfare threatens the obliteration of human life on a previously unimaginable scale. The sense of awe and "fear of the Lord" which former generations felt in approaching these issues weighs upon us with new urgency.[7]

The significance of this religious belief in a divine creation was stated well by Walter Stein, who pointed out that "much of the nuclear debate within the Church is concerned with comparisons of risks—the prudential balancing of the risks of a nuclear war against the risks of being subjugated by a totalitarian opponent. These are also the main terms in which secular thinking seeks to assess these matters." But for the one who believes in a God who alone is the Lord of all creation, the threat to the whole created order contained in our nuclear arsenal is "the ultimate blasphemy." As Mr. Stein made clear, "even if, statistically, the risks of a nuclear conflagration could reasonably be regarded as small—and who could provide decisive grounds for such a judgment?—the absoluteness of the risks thus still accepted would remain absolutely prohibitive morally."[8] In fact, of course, the more we develop our nuclear arsenal as our strategy of deterrence demands, the more we expose all of creation to the ultimate threat and participate in this ultimate blasphemy. The very dynamic quality of deterrence that demands that both sides match each other weapon for weapon, and weapon system for weapon system, is pushing us closer and closer to the point at which we will bring about the end of the world as we know it.

In a very sobering article, Leslie H. Gelb, the national security correspondent for the *New York Times,* alerted us to the fact that

> the United States and the Soviet Union now are on the threshold of decisions that could make nuclear war seriously thinkable for the first time. In 10 to 15 years, new technologies now being developed and tested could, if deployed, fundamentally and irretrievably undermine

the basic philosophy that has been the center of both sides' nuclear strategy—mutual deterrence. If the go-ahead is given to deploy these new technologies, a Soviet or American military planner could, before the end of this century, be able to make all of the following statements to his leader for the first time:

"We can blind all their satellites, destroy their capital in five or six minutes, before they can react, and, with a few well-placed nuclear airbursts, we can knock out their whole communications network and make them sightless and headless."

"With new pinpoint-accurate missile warheads, I can guarantee that we can destroy virtually every missile in a silo, every submarine in port, and every bomber on an airfield. That will leave our adversaries only with missiles in their submarines at sea, and we are now able to locate and neutralize this ultimate retaliatory threat. Almost all of their few remaining missiles can be destroyed by our missile defense system."

"We may suffer a few million casualties, but our adversary will be thoroughly and finally defeated. And if we don't do it to him now, it is he who will be able to win by striking the first blow."

As Mr. Gelb went on to point out, "the overriding question for leaders in Moscow and Washington is: Can they manage these mounting nuclear threats?"[9]

But the overriding moral question, especially in view of these rapid and ever more dangerous developments in the nuclear arms race, is: Can it ever be right to expose the world and the whole human species, as well as other species, to extinction? Must not the Church denounce such threats to the created order as the ultimate blasphemy?

A second reason why the strategy of deterrence is morally flawed becomes clear when we begin to compute what it costs to maintain this strategy and the arms race that is the result. Aware of these huge costs, the bishops of the world at Vatican Council II condemned the arms race as "one of the greatest curses on the human race" and went on to say, "the harm it inflicts on the poor is more than can be endured." In our pastoral letter we make clear that "the fact of a massive distortion of resources in the face of crying human need creates a moral question."[10]

It is not difficult to document the extent of poverty in today's world. At the end of 1983 there were about 35 million people in the United States who, by the government's official definition, were poor. Another 20 to 30 million had so little that by any reasonable standard they were also needy. After a decline in the annual rate of poverty from 14.7 percent in 1966 to 11.7 percent in 1979, the figure climbed to 15.2 percent by the end of 1983. In the four years between 1979 and 1983 the number of those living in poverty in the United States increased by over 9 million people. During this same period the number of poor children under the age of six jumped by 51 percent.[11]

These figures tell only part of the story of hardship in the United States. One need look no further than the major cities to see examples of homelessness and hunger. Poor people, including many former mental patients released from state hospitals, roam the streets, ill-clad and sleeping in doorways or on subway grates at night. No one knows how many homeless people there are now, but estimates run from 250,000 to 3 million.[12] The striking rise in poverty has also led to problems for many in obtaining enough food. In the early 1980s the number of people seeking emergency food aid went up dramatically at agencies that provide such assistance.[13] Newspapers regularly chronicle the details of human beings forced to stand in line at soup kitchens because they have no other way of feeding themselves. The effects of improper nutrition are particularly damaging to small children, whose growth may be stunted and whose mental development may be impaired. In late 1983 the Massachusetts Department of Public Health reported that nearly one in five of the low-income children it surveyed was either stunted, abnormally underweight, or anemic. Similar studies in other areas have found comparable results.[14]

When we look beyond the United States to the less-developed countries, we find an even more distressing situation.

- 800 million people in less-developed countries live in conditions of absolute poverty, "a condition of life so limited by malnutrition, illiteracy, disease, high infant mortality, and low life expectancy as to be beneath any rational definition of human decency."[15]
- Half of the world's population—2.26 billion people—live in countries in which the per capita annual income is the equivalent of $400 or less (U.S. per capita income is $12,530).[16]
- 450 million people are malnourished or facing starvation, despite abundant harvests worldwide.[17]
- 15 out of every 100 children born in these countries will die before the age of five, and hundreds of thousands of the survivors will be stunted physically or mentally.
- 40,000 children die every day from hunger-related causes.
- The average life expectancy of these people (except for the People's Republic of China) is forty-eight years (in the United States it is seventy-four years).[18]

These numbers give us some sense of the situation in which the vast majority of the world's people live. But the numbers cannot adequately portray the tragic desperation of these people. They can only highlight the scandal of such a situation in a 12-trillion-dollar world economy, of which our economy accounts for more than one-fourth.[19]

In 1976, in preparation for the first special session on disarmament sponsored by the United Nations, the Vatican submitted a paper. It contained this statement: "The arms race is to be condemned unreservedly. Why? Because it's an injustice. Even if the weapons are never used, the arms race itself is an act of aggression against the poor, causing them to starve."[20] You may think that's an exaggeration. I do not. I think that we deliberately choose how we will use our resources, and we choose to let fifteen children die every minute while we build up weapons that can only lead to our ultimate destruction.

Pope John Paul II, in his first encyclical letter, made a judgment about this situation. He said, "We all know well that the areas of misery and hunger on our globe could have been made fertile in a short time if gigantic investments for armaments at the service of war and destruction had been changed into investments for food at the service of life."[21] "We all know well. . . ." And yet, we continue to choose armaments of death and destruction. Isn't there something terribly evil in that? Again we are faced with an overriding moral question: Can it be right, in the face of such widespread and tragic human need, to misappropriate the resources of the earth to build weapons that will only destroy?

The third and most compelling argument to demonstrate the very serious moral problem with the strategy of deterrence is based on the intention inherent in that strategy to kill indiscriminately and on a scale that would exceed anything that has ever happened in the history of the world. As Walter Stein stated in his article,

the logic of intention is very direct and simple. By the declarations which they make, and by their actual strategic preparations—weapons mix, weapons deployment and targeting plans—governments indicate willingness, if deterrence fails, to use these weapons in warfare.

But could not a government decide to confine itself to a "bluff"— mere possession of weapons, without making threats, or making threats but with no intention of every carrying them out? There are no grounds for thinking that any government with nuclear capacity has ever considered such a course.[22]

That this is clearly the case is evident from the experience of those involved in executing the nuclear-deterrent threat. Francis X. Winters, a moral theologian from Georgetown University, wrote about a military friend.

> I would nevertheless ask [you] to meditate a while on a conversation I had some years ago with a retired United States military officer who had once been charged with the responsibility of executing the deterrent threat in the event the presidential command-center were destroyed. Chatting over a gracious dinner at his retirement home, the officer discussed his former responsibilities: "If the responsibility fell to me, I fully intended to destroy the Soviet Union."

> A stillness fell over the dinner table as his family and I tried to assimilate this articulation of Christian political responsibility. Even today as I write, these words echo resoundingly. They are not abstract. Nor are they singular. Every officer who assumes a position in the chain of command must first say these words to himself (and undoubtedly to his superiors).[23]

It is abundantly clear that the strategy of deterrence includes the clear intention to do evil, the most horrendous evil. And because sin is in the intention, we are already deeply involved in a most terrible kind of sin because of our nuclear deterrence strategy.

It is most important to remember that it is not just every officer in a military chain of command who bears the responsibility for this intention. All of us, as taxpayers and as citizens, share in the responsibility for the public policies of our nation. We are in a situation where we as a people are saying we fully intend to do an evil that exceeds anything that has ever happened in the world; to destroy hundreds of millions of people; to bring about what the scientists call a "nuclear winter," a situation in which there will be darkness over the whole earth, temperatures below freezing so that life cannot be sustained—the end of the world. "I fully intend to do it."

Perhaps we didn't perceive this or intend this when the strategy of deterrence was first devised so many years ago. But here we are today, caught in this terrible evil, the misuse of our resources and the intention to do destruction to life and even to the world, on a scale that is beyond our power to imagine. Now that we perceive clearly the moral dilemma that confronts us, perhaps we also understand the reason for the bishops' judgment that deterrence is morally acceptable *in a strictly conditioned way*. Cardinal Basil Hume, writing in the *Times* (London), put it well: "There is a tension

... between the moral imperative not to use such inhuman weapons and a policy of nuclear deterrence with its declared willingness to use them if attacked. To condemn all use and yet to accept deterrence places us in a seemingly contradictory position." In such a situation, he goes on to insist, "To retain moral credibility, however, there must be a firm and effective intention to extricate ourselves from the present fearful situation as quickly as possible."[24]

The possibility of nuclear war may be much closer than we realize. The lack of success in arms control negotiations combined with the tendency on the part of our national leaders (and presumably the leaders of the Soviet Union as well) to interpret every local conflict, no matter how remote, as an episode in a world confrontation between competing ideologies presents a situation ripe for explosion. In the context of an arms race that seems to have developed a dynamic of its own, all that is needed is a rash misjudgment or accident to serve as detonator for the final holocaust. As Christians we cannot be indifferent to the danger to the planet and its inhabitants, but our first and most pressing concern is the moral dimension—the fact that by our actions (or inaction!) we may bear the responsibility and guilt for the intentional destruction of God's creation.

The pastoral letter shows us the way to escape this evil of the destruction of the world and the awesome responsibility and guilt for this indescribable sin: by insisting that the two strict conditions for the moral acceptance of deterrence be fulfilled. Our obligation as loyal Americans, committed to acting in a morally acceptable way, is clear. We must do everything possible to save creation from destruction at the hands of God's creatures. This means changing our policies—and, if need be, personnel—responsible for the atmosphere of increasing tension and animosity. In keeping with the conditions put forth in the pastoral letter, these policies must be replaced by serious and sincere decisions to end our continuing escalation of the production and deployment of new weapons, to end our quest for nuclear superiority and the capability to wage nuclear warfare. In addition, genuine, even bold steps must be taken to move toward progressive disarmament. Such steps will help to create that spirit of mutual trust that, as Pope John XXIII told us, is the *only* sure basis for a just and lasting peace on earth.

Forty years ago the distinguished Catholic University scholar, Monsignor Paul Hanly Furfey, published his book *The Mystery of Iniquity.* A sociologist, he reminded his readers that all social problems— economic injustice, racism, violence, and war—are evidence of the activity of supernatural evil in human affairs.[25] His was not an argument for resignation or submission; instead, it was an inspirational call for greater efforts as followers of Christ to counteract the Satanic influence that finds expression in the actions of often well intentioned human instruments. There is perhaps no better illustration of Furfey's hypothesis than the threat of nuclear annihilation.

Diabolical in its origins or not, the power to unleash the final holocaust is now ours. Though time is running out, it is not too late to call a halt and come to terms with the truth that this power may not be used. The bishops' pastoral letter is a major help in bringing people to that truth. Now each of us must carry on the work of the pastoral. We must speak this truth and act on it.

NOTES

The text of this chapter is adapted from a lecture presented by the author at the University of California at Santa Barbara, 26 February 1985.

1. U.S. Catholic Bishops, *Challenge of Peace, God's Promise and Our Response: A Pastoral Letter on War and Peace* (Ramsey, N.J.: Paulist Press, 1983).

2. Ibid., par. 186.

3. Ibid., par. 187.

4. Ibid., par. 188.

5. Ibid., pars. 197, 198.

6. Ibid., par. 175.

7. Ibid.

8. Walter Stein, "The Case Against Deterrence," *The Tablet* 238 (London, 27 October 1984).

9. Leslie H. Gelb, "Is the Nuclear Threat Manageable?" *New York Times Magazine* 133, no. 45 (4 March 1984):26–36, 65, 80, 92.

10. U.S. Catholic Bishops, *Challenge of Peace,* par. 270.

11. U.S., Bureau of the Census, *Money Income and Poverty Status of Families and Persons in the United States: 1983,* Current Population Reports, Series P-60, no. 145 (Washington, D.C.: U.S. Government Printing Office, 1984), p. 20.

12. U.S., Department of Housing and Urban Development, Office of Policy Development and Research, *A Report to the Secretary on the Homeless and Emergency Shelters* (Washington, D.C.: U.S. Government Printing Office, May 1984); Mary Ellen Hombs and Mitch Snyder, *Homelessness in America: A Forced March to Nowhere* (Washington, D.C.: Community for Creative Non-Violence, December 1982).

13. *Soup Lines and Food Baskets: A Survey of Increased Participation in Emergency Food Programs* (Washington, D.C.: Center on Budget and Policy Priorities, May 1983), pp. 5–6; *Status Report: Emergency Food, Shelter, and Energy Programs in 20 Cities* (Washington, D.C.: U.S. Conference of Mayors, January 1984), p. 2.

14. *Massachusetts Nutrition Survey* (Boston: Massachusetts Department of Public Health, 1983).

15. Robert S. McNamara, "Address to the Board of Governors of the World Bank," 30 September 1980, Washington, D.C. World Bank President McNamara expressed this view repeatedly in similar language at the annual meeting of the bank's board.

16. Overseas Development Council, *U.S. Policy and the Third World: Agenda 1983* (New York: Praeger, 1983), Table C-3.

17. There are numerous sources for figures between 435 million and 500 million. See United Nations, Food and Agriculture Organization, *Dimensions of Need* (Rome, 1982), p. E9.

18. *World Development Report,* 1984, Table 23.

19. Overseas Development Council, *U.S. Policy and the Third World.*

20. 1976 Vatican paper.

21. John Paul II, *Redeemer of Man* (*Redemptor Hominis*) (Washington, D.C.: Catholic Conference, 1979), par. 16.

22. Stein, "The Case Against Deterrence," p. 1048.

23. Francis X. Winters, "Catholic Debate and Division on Deterrence," *America* 147, no. 7 (18 September 1982):127–131.

24. Cardinal Basil Hume, "Towards a Nuclear Morality," *Times* (London, 17 November 1983), p. 12.

25. Paul Hanly Furfey, *The Mystery of Iniquity* (Milwaukee, Wis.: Bruce Publishing Company, 1944, second printing 1945).

ABBREVIATIONS

ABM   antiballistic missile
ACDA   Arms Control and Disarmament Agency
ALCM   air-launched cruise missile
ASAT   antisatellite system

BMD   ballistic missile defense

CDE   Conference on Disarmament in Europe (Conference on
            Confidence- and Security-Building Measures in Europe)
CEP   circular probable error
C³I   Command, Control, Communications, and Intelligence
CIA   Central Intelligence Agency
CSCE   Conference on Security and Cooperation in Europe

DARPA   Defense Advanced Research Projects Agency
DNA   Defense Nuclear Agency
DOD   Department of Defense

EMP   electromagnetic pulse

FRG   Federal Republic of Germany

GDR   German Democratic Republic
GLCM   ground-launched cruise missile

HOE   Homing Overlay Experiment

ICBM   intercontinental ballistic missile
INF   intermediate-range nuclear force
IOC   initial operational capability

JCS	Joint Chiefs of Staff
LODE	Large Optics Demonstration Experiment
MAD	mutual assured destruction
MBFR	Mutual and Balanced Force Reductions
MHV	Miniature Homing Vehicle
MIRV	multiple independently targetable reentry vehicle
MPS	multiple protective shelters
MRBM	medium-range ballistic missile
MX	missile experimental
NATO	North Atlantic Treaty Organization
NCA	National Command Authority
NPT	Nuclear Non-Proliferation Treaty
OSD	Office of the Secretary of Defense
PSAC	President's Science Advisory Committee
PTB	Partial Test Ban Treaty
RV	reentry vehicle
SALT	Strategic Arms Limitation Talks
SDI	Strategic Defense Initiative ("Star Wars" plan)
SLBM	submarine-launched ballistic missile
SLCM	sea-launched cruise missile
SST	supersonic transport
START	Strategic Arms Reduction Talks
TNF	Theater Nuclear Forces
UN	United Nations
USSR	Union of Soviet Socialist Republics

ABOUT THE EDITOR
AND CONTRIBUTORS

Wolfram F. Hanrieder is professor of political science at the University of California, Santa Barbara, and chairman of the Advisory Committee, Program on Global Peace and Security. He has written numerous books and articles on the transatlantic alliance, West German and West European foreign policies, and national security policy and arms control. His publications include *Arms Control and Security: Current Issues* (editor; Westview, 1979).

Ernst-Otto Czempiel is professor of international relations at the University of Frankfurt and a director of its Peace Research Institute. He has written numerous books and articles on peace research, U.S. and German foreign policy, and the theory of international politics.

Jonathan Dean, now arms control adviser of the Union of Concerned Scientists, was U.S. representative to the NATO–Warsaw Pact Force Reduction Negotiations in Vienna (the MBFR talks) between 1978 and 1981, having served as deputy U.S. representative from the beginning of these talks in 1973. He was deputy U.S. negotiator in the 1971 Four Power Berlin Agreement with the Soviet Union.

Kurt Gottfried teaches physics at Cornell University. He has served on the High Energy Physics Advisory Panel, on the National Research Council of Canada, and on the Board of Directors of the Union of Concerned Scientists. He has written or coauthored over fifty scientific journal articles and review papers.

Bishop Thomas Gumbleton was a member of the Bishop's Conference that drafted the pastoral letter "Challenge of Peace, God's Promise and Our Response" in 1983. He went to Vietnam in 1973 to investigate the situation of political prisoners and traveled to Iran in 1979 as a representative of the National Conference of Catholic Bishops to visit the Americans held hostage.

Robert A. Hoover is professor of political science and dean of the College of Humanities, Arts, and Social Sciences at Utah State University. His writings include *Arms Control: The Interwar Naval Limitations Agreements* (1979); *MX Controversy: A Guide to Issues and References* (1982); and (with Lauren H. Holland) *The MX Decision: A New Direction in U.S. Weapons Procurement Policy?* (Westview, 1985).

Richard Ned Lebow is professor of government and director of the Peace Studies Program, Cornell University. He was a member of the study panel of the Union of Concerned Scientists on "Space-Based Missile Defense." His publications include *Between Peace and War: The Nature of International Crisis* (1981); *White Britain and Black Ireland: The Influence of Stereotypes on Colonial Policy* (1976); and (with Gregory Henderson and John Stoessinger) *Divided Nations in a Divided World* (1974).

Paul C. Warnke was director of the U.S. Arms Control and Disarmament Agency (1977–1978) and served as chief negotiator for the United States in the Strategic Arms Limitation Treaty talks. He has also served as general counsel for the Department of Defense and as assistant secretary of defense for international security affairs. He practices law in Washington, D.C.

Herbert York is professor of physics at the University of California, San Diego, and director of the University of California's statewide Institute on Global Conflict and Cooperation. Dr. York worked on the Manhattan Project, initiated and directed the Lawrence Livermore Laboratory, and was the first chief scientist of the Advanced Research Projects Agency. From 1961 to 1964 he was chancellor at the University of California, San Diego. Dr. York has served as a member of the U.S. delegation to the U.S.-Soviet ASAT Arms Control Talks (1978–1979) and as U.S. ambassador to the Comprehensive Test Ban negotiations in Geneva (1978–1981). His publications include *Race to Oblivion* (1971); *The Advisors: Oppenheimer, Teller, and the Superbomb* (1976); and *Arms Control* (editor, 1973).